8/17 Pa

Praise for *The Innovation Code*

"You know what I never want to do again? Be in a meeting about another meeting. It's the business leaders' opportunity and responsibility to create a culture that catalyzes, identifies, and cultivates innovators—the lifeblood of any organization. Meetings aren't the answer; it's innovation. *The Innovation Code* provides clear guidance on how to identify innovation and get the best from it."
—**Victoria R. Montgomery-Brown, CEO and cofounder, Big Think**

"It is rare to find a senior executive at a large company who does not claim to value innovation; however, ask him for his 'innovation playbook' and you will likely get a blank stare. In *The Innovation Code*, Professor Jeff DeGraff has written the definitive guide to creating the right conditions, assembling and nurturing the right team, and recognizing and harnessing the right interpersonal conflicts to create a winning innovation culture. *The Innovation Code* is itself a conflict—a well-written book of ideas that nonetheless can be readily put into practice by managers who want to innovate for growth."
—**Tom Glocer, former CEO, Thomson Reuters**

"With *The Innovation Code*, Jeff DeGraff masterfully reveals the personality traits that drive innovation and shows us how we can harness those traits in our organizations, our teams, and ourselves."
—**Aaron Fried, Vice President, MetLife**

"*The Innovation Code* should be a 'must' for leaders who wish their organizations to grow and prosper. The essence of the book, as its title suggests, is the acceptance—first by the leader and then by her or his close associates—of the fact that conflict, disruption, and challenge of the status quo are a healthy proposition and the basis for innovation to occur and for the organization to gain strength from it. When this concept is embraced, the environment is poised to move forward, but to do so, it needs the balance of creativity, control, competition, and understanding that comes from a diverse workforce. The book explains in simple and understandable ways the four competing approaches that drive innovation and thereby growth. Jeff DeGraff beautifully describes the creative power of constructive conflict, something that can be applied to manufacturing as well as service industries the world over."
—**Carlos A. Pellegrini, MD, FACS, Chief Medical Officer, UW Medicine; Vice President for Medical Affairs, University of Washington; and former President, American College of Surgeons**

"Jeff DeGraff has helped many of the world's leading arts organizations summon the courage to evolve, adapt, and develop new ways to grow their organizations. Conflict is an honest and necessary part of leading any successful arts and entertainment organization. *The Innovation Code* should be standard issue for anyone who is a leader in the arts!"
—**Matthew VanBesien, President, New York Philharmonic**

"The idea of creative tension has been around for many years. The difficulty comes with how to keep it positive, manage it, and take advantage of the outcomes. Jeff's expertise is born of his experience with hundreds of companies around the globe. His practical insights and advice will help you harness the power of diversity and creativity and build a culture to maximize innovation."

—**Mabel Casey, Vice President, Global Marketing and Sales Support, Haworth, Inc.**

"Innovation is hard. Unlike other books, *The Innovation Code* doesn't gloss over it or make it sound easy. In fact, it tackles the hardest element: how to create constructive conflict and use it to innovate. In this book, DeGraff, the Dean of Innovation, shares his insights from working with many organizations to create a practical guide for all students of innovation."

—**Mark Thompson, *New York Times* bestselling author, *Forbes* columnist, and venture capitalist**

"Most companies want a culture of innovation, but they don't know what it is or how to develop one. DeGraff shows us what we need to do in the most fundamental way: adopting the mindset of innovator and embracing gracious conflicts. Instead of avoiding conflicts, DeGraff explains that innovators can harness this energy to create something better and new. This book is a playbook about innovation that can be applied in any field."

—**Tan Le, founder and CEO, EMOTIV**

"*The Innovation Code* shows you how to play to win the innovation game. Whether you're managing a professional sports team, or any other kind of organization, or just trying to develop your own skills, *The Innovation Code* is the playbook for you."

—**R. C. Buford, General Manager, San Antonio Spurs**

THE
INNOVATION
CODE

THE
INNOVATION
CODE

THE
CREATIVE POWER
OF CONSTRUCTIVE
CONFLICT

JEFF DEGRAFF

THE DEAN OF INNOVATION

AND STANEY DEGRAFF

BK

Berrett–Koehler Publishers, Inc.
a BK Business book

Berrett-Koehler Publishers, Inc.
1333 Broadway, Suite 1000
Oakland, CA 94612-1921
Tel: (510) 817-2277
Fax: (510) 817-2278
www.bkconnection.com

Ordering Information
Quantity sales. Special discounts are available on quantity purchases by corporations, associations, and others. For details, contact the "Special Sales Department" at the Berrett-Koehler address above.
Individual sales. Berrett-Koehler publications are available through most bookstores. They can also be ordered directly from Berrett-Koehler: Tel: (800) 929-2929; Fax: (802) 864-7626; www.bkconnection.com
Orders for college textbook/course adoption use. Please contact Berrett-Koehler: Tel: (800) 929-2929; Fax: (802) 864-7626.
Orders by U.S. trade bookstores and wholesalers. Please contact Ingram Publisher Services, Tel: (800) 509-4887; Fax: (800) 838-1149; E-mail: customer.service@ingrampublisherservices.com; or visit www.ingrampublisherservices.com/Ordering for details about electronic ordering.

Berrett-Koehler and the BK logo are registered trademarks of Berrett-Koehler Publishers, Inc.

Printed in the United States of America

Berrett-Koehler books are printed on long-lasting acid-free paper. When it is available, we choose paper that has been manufactured by environmentally responsible processes. These may include using trees grown in sustainable forests, incorporating recycled paper, minimizing chlorine in bleaching, or recycling the energy produced at the paper mill.

Library of Congress Cataloging-in-Publication Data

Names: DeGraff, Jeffrey Thomas, author. | DeGraff, Staney, author.
Title: The innovation code : the creative power of constructive conflict / by Jeff DeGraff and Staney DeGraff.
Description: First edition | Oakland, California : Berrett-Koehler Publishers, [2017] | Includes bibliographical references.
Identifiers: LCCN 2017007385 | ISBN 9781523084760 (hardcover)
Subjects: LCSH: Organizational change. | Organizational behavior. | Creative ability in business.
Classification: LCC HD58.8 .D4382 2017 | DDC 658.4/063--dc23
LC record available at https://lccn.loc.gov/2017007385

ISBN: 978-1-5230-8476-0

23 22 21 20 19 18 17   5 4 3 2 1

Cover Design: Rob Johnson, Toprotype, Inc.
Book Production: Adept Content Solutions

This book is dedicated to the late
Budi Dharmakusuma (Yap Chuan Yu),
an entrepreneur, educator, and loving father,
who believed in the creative power of diverse
communities to overcome poverty,
disability, and prejudice.

Contents

Preface

The discord in the early moments of a brainstorming session is like a symphony: the tense back and forth between wildly different thinkers, the points of antagonistic contact between totally opposing worldviews. When it comes to any innovation initiative —from building the next breakthrough app to designing the next miracle drug—disharmony is crucial. The only way to create new hybrid solutions is to clash. Innovation happens when we bring people with contrasting perspectives and complementary areas of expertise together in one room. Innovation is unlike any other form of value or growth because it's the only kind that necessitates discomfort. It requires us to *not* get along. We innovate when we disrupt, and we first have to disrupt each other. It's best that we innovate not with people we agree with but with people who will challenge us. Forget everything you've ever heard about teamwork and harmony. It's time to ruffle some feathers.

This is precisely what the *The Innovation Code: The Creative Power of Constructive Conflict* is about. This book introduces a simple framework to explain the way different kinds of thinkers and leaders can create constructive conflict in any organization. There are four fundamental kinds of innovators. Each of these innovators holds dear a different value proposition, which guides the way each thinks and acts. Understanding how these four kinds interact and work against each other will help you facilitate innovation in your organization and life. This book is derived from our experience in working with nearly 200 of the Fortune 500 companies across the globe, jumpstarting creative growth in a variety of fields from healthcare to entertainment to manufacturing. With this book, we've distilled our years of experience into a clear, step-by-step guide to navigating innovation teams and harnessing the energy of constructive conflict.

The Innovation Code contains the interactions between the four basic approaches to innovation, represented by the four different kinds of dominant worldviews or value propositions in any business. There's the wild experimentation of the **Artist**, the pragmatic caution of the **Engineer**, the quick competitiveness of the **Athlete**, and the patient community building of the **Sage**.

The four dominant worldviews come together to produce a positive tension, a constructive conflict that generates sustainable growth. When outside-the-box Artists clash with by-the-book Engineers, the result is innovation that's simultaneously revolutionary and sensible. When aggressive, profit-hungry Athletes clash with empathic, high-minded Sages, the result is innovation that's at once winning and conscientious.

Preface

This book shows you how each of these four types functions and how to build, manage, and embrace the dynamic discord of a team that contains all four elements of the Innovation Code. There is a short assessment that you can take at the end of Chapter 2 to see how you fit into the four types. Please see The Innovation Code Supplemental Material section on page 129 for more information about online assessments and other supporting materials. But for now, it's time to get uncomfortable, to talk to people you don't agree with, to collaborate with thinkers who might otherwise be your rivals, even your enemies. Let's get disruptive.

CHAPTER 1

Tell Me Your Biggest Weakness

Tell me your biggest weakness: it's that awful, cringe-worthy question anyone inside or outside of corporate America will immediately recognize as the most overused, clichéd line in the job interview script. "I work so hard I tire myself out," you've probably once said. Or, even better: "I'm too much of a perfectionist." You groan—we all groan—because the very premise of the question is absurd. Why would anyone give away their worst quality at the moment when they're supposed to be at their best?

Take a step outside of the interview room, and the question evokes a sense of dread. Its real absurdity is its sheer difficulty. How are you supposed to articulate a legitimate vulnerability in the space of a two-minute conclusion to a conversation with someone you've never met? Then there's the haunting suspicion that there might be a real answer to the question that you don't even know yourself. Is it possible to know what's great about you without also knowing what's not so great?

It's a wonder that the most popular interview question of all time is actually a good question—despite the fact that most likely it never yielded a meaningful answer in the history of hiring. That's because it's pretty damn hard. And even understanding why it's hard is, well, hard.

What makes it so hard to answer that question is ourselves: because we're clouded by our own biases and worldviews, it's nearly (though not totally) impossible to get outside of our heads and get an objective look at what's wrong with us. This bias is our dominant worldview.

The Upside and Downside of Your Dominant Worldview

On the one hand, your dominant worldview is your biggest strength—the quality that makes you stand out from other people. Your dominant worldview determines the way you approach all challenges in your life. Some people are big-picture thinkers. Others fixate on particulars. Some people are pragmatic and by the book when it comes to solving problems. Others are dreamers who go outside the box. Some people are goal-oriented, driven by the thrill of competition. Others are patient listeners, inspired by a cooperative community that they build around them. These dominant worldviews are our greatest gifts, the set of skills we bring to any situation.

On the other hand, your dominant worldview is holding you back. Your defining quality is also your greatest weakness. The problem is that our dominant worldviews overpower all other points of view. Our dominant worldviews are so intense that we lose the ability to think outside of them. They give us blind spots. We become prisoners of our own ideology. Left by themselves, the pragmatic thinkers become bureaucrats. The big-picture thinkers become chaotic. The goal-oriented thinkers become control freaks. The patient thinkers become irrationally enthusiastic.

The biggest obstacle you face on the path to innovation is yourself. Dominant worldviews of all kinds can distort reality. They inevitably twist facts and prevent us from seeing the bigger picture. When it comes to innovation, our dominant worldviews impede creative thinking. The most effective innovation solutions are almost always hybrids, processes that combine multiple perspectives, so it's imperative that we learn to break free of our own biases and preconceptions.

You Are Your Own
Biggest Problem

Consider this tale of a whiz kid fresh out of graduate school, hired as an operating officer for a rapidly growing company. In the wake of wild success, he unexpectedly found that things weren't getting done. When he confided in his boss, he claimed that the problems were with the people he managed..But the CEO told him that what they all had in common was him. He was the source of his own problem.

"Ask everyone on your team what you're incompetent at," the CEO said. And he did. One by one, they told him what he couldn't do. "You're not very good with finances," one said. "Marketing just isn't your thing," another said. When he went back to his boss, the CEO told him they were all correct. "Well, they're right. Now make other people do all those things so you can have the time to do what you're best at—which is, of course, strategy. No one can come up with solutions to complicated problems like you can." Over time, the whiz kid learned to delegate. He learned to accept his weaknesses and acknowledge his strengths. He learned to rely on the talents of others as he showcased his own talent.

What Are the Gifts You Don't Know You Have?

To break free of your dominant worldview is also to embrace it. And sometimes embracing it is even harder—because we can't always see what we have to offer the world. Take as an example the story of Miriam.

Miriam was a caretaker to everyone but herself. She was always quick with a pleasant word or a comforting comment that made you believe everything was going to be just fine. Few would have suspected that this middle-aged woman with the radiant smile had more worries than most. It all started out well enough for Miriam. She graduated from college and married her high school sweetheart. But twenty-five years later, he ran out on her and their five children. Though her career as a nurse brought her tremendous satisfaction, it didn't provide much in the way of income. Miriam struggled just to make it all work, and it did, for a while. As if on cue, after all of her children had grown and moved out of the house, her vivacious mother was diagnosed with dementia. Always a deeply spiritual person, she went to her rabbi seeking advice. He was very helpful, and with the support of her synagogue, her mother was moved to a local assisted living center where Miriam could visit her daily.

Believing that Miriam's situation was becoming more common among members of his congregation, the rabbi asked Miriam to tell her personal story at temple one Friday evening. She was reluctant to speak to her friends and neighbors about such a deeply personal and difficult subject. But the rabbi emphasized that other members of the synagogue needed her help to get through their own struggles. So when the appointed time came, Miriam slowly began to disclose the challenges of her life and how she had, to the best of her abilities, endeavored to meet them through prayer and positive action. What followed were drawn-out moments of silence and sobbing. When the services were complete, dozens of congregation members came up to talk to Miriam. To her surprise, many of them wanted to share their own experiences with parents who needed assistance in their golden years. The rabbi suggested that Miriam develop an educational program that could be delivered at other synagogues and perhaps beyond.

At the medical center where Miriam worked, she talked with a wide array of doctors, nurses, patients, and their families to better understand the key challenges, potential solutions, and the needs of caretakers. She met with specialists who were happy to share their expertise and information. Over the course of a year, Miriam became a practical expert on caring for elderly parents with dementia. She was asked to speak at temples, nursing homes, and hospices. With each new speech, Miriam added to her material—stories others had given her, variations on her subject matter, handouts, and even a website filled with articles and other resources.

These days, Miriam is widely known as a regular on the speaking circuit. It all came together the moment she realized what she had to offer to the people around her. She had powerful gifts of storytelling, caregiving, empathy, communication, and bringing groups together, but it wasn't until she'd been put in this difficult—indeed, dire—situation that she knew she had them.

What are the gifts you don't know you have? That's precisely the question this book will help you answer.

Introducing the
Innovation Code

The Innovation Code is a system for identifying, understanding, and combining the different dominant worldviews of creative thinkers and leaders. A worldview is more than a type or a style. It's a collection of deeply held beliefs about how we interpret and experience the world. A dominant worldview is a comprehensive conception of the world from a specific standpoint. We derive these views from our personal experiences as well as the cultures in which we are socialized, for we are neither self-contained nor self-created. We exist as part of a larger community and system. Our dominant worldview may change over time as we experience new situations and become more self-aware of our own inclinations.

In revealing your greatest strength, your dominant worldview also reveals your greatest weakness. Furthermore, it considers how each kind of thinker and leader interacts with others, so you can determine the other people you need to surround yourself with most. The best innovation teams are like bands of superheroes: each member acknowledges and makes use of his or her gifts and talents, but they don't let those superpowers limit them. They use them at the appropriate moments and then stand back and let their partners take over at other moments.

There are four basic approaches to innovation: the Artist, who loves radical innovation; the Engineer, who constantly improves everything; the Athlete, who competes to develop the best innovation; and the Sage, who innovates through collaboration. These approaches come together to produce a positive tension, a constructive conflict that promotes sustainable and scalable growth. When you combine the radical, visionary thinking of the Artist and the methodical, practical thinking of the Engineer, you get innovation that's both revolutionary and manageable, highly ambitious but without high risk. When you combine the cutthroat, results-oriented attitude of the Athlete with the conscientious, values-oriented attitude of the Sage, you get innovation that's both a good investment and good for the world.

In today's snappy corporate speak, forms of creative leadership are like statement blazers or ultra low-rise jeans: they're either in or they're out. Every year, the most popular business magazines claim that a certain type of person is the most innovative of the moment. This month, it might be the triumph of the technological guru. In the fall, it might be the rise of the artistic genius. Pundits treat innovation strategies as if they were fashion trends, hot during one season, only to become passé the next.

The truth is that dominant worldviews are more than just catchy buzzwords on a glossy list. There is no single approach to innovation that will always come out on top. There is no overriding trend you can rely on. Rather, knowing which kinds of leaders to bring to your project is about knowing all the things you can't do yourself.

Innovation Is
Not About Alignment

Most people like to surround themselves with people who are like them and run the plays that they're used to running. But in reality, it's crucial to work with people who have different skills than you and to run a wide variety of plays in order to increase the likelihood that one of them will work.

Do things that make you feel uncomfortable. Talk to people with whom you have nothing in common. Remember that the ideal solutions to the most complicated problems will never involve just one mode of thinking. They always require a cross-boundary, interdisciplinary approach that takes advantage of multiple—and often seemingly contradictory—mindsets and ranges of skills.

Innovation is not about alignment. It is about constructive conflict—positive tension. This is exactly how and where innovation happens: you need to surround yourself with people who are not like you.

The Innovation Code begins with a look at yourself: both what you have to offer the world and how you fit into that world. Once we've established a structure of the self, we'll discuss how you can create constructive conflicts. We'll go through each of the four innovation types individually, examining all of their talents and flaws, their gifts and shortcomings, and talk about how these types use constructive conflict to innovate. Finally, we'll end with an action plan for the future, a set of simple tools for building and maintaining an innovative mindset and an ever-evolving sense of self.

So that question we've all sighed, rolled our eyes at, and thought we were done with forever once that interview ended is actually the start of something great. For identifying your biggest weakness is the first step to looking outward and seeing the kinds of people to enlist on your teams. Think of the question as less of a demand than an exchange: Tell me your biggest weakness and I'll give you my greatest strength.

Summary

Innovation starts with two self-assessments—one devastating, the other uplifting: what's the worst part about yourself and the best part about yourself. Once you've really identified your greatest weaknesses and strengths, you can determine what kind of people you need to surrounded yourself with. Find people who are un-like you, who can push you to create the things you can't on your own. Create your own team of superheroes.

Exercise

Start your journey toward growth by looking closer at the stories you tell about yourself. For it's in these self-narratives—the stories we tell ourselves—where we can get the strongest idea of our strengths and weaknesses.

1. Reflect on your story

Draw a straight line on a page. Treat this as a timeline of your life. Starting at the right end, which represents today, recall memorable events working backwards. List them on your timeline. This doesn't mean recalling every important event but rather whichever events feel significant to you right now: perhaps an argument with a sibling, a decision not to take a job, or a project that really made your career. Give yourself a moment to reflect on these events.

2. Analyze a moment of failure

Now pick one event that represents a failure: a bad relationship, a work of art never completed, a job from which you were fired. Recall the event with as much detail as possible: who, what, where, when, why, and how.

Make sense of this failure. Ask yourself these questions: What went wrong? Why? What went right? Why? Have you experienced similar failures in the past? Do you see a pattern? What does this tell you about your biggest weakness?

3. Analyze a moment of success

Now, repeat this self-assessment by reflecting on a story of success. Ask yourself the same questions you asked about your failure. What do these complementary self-narratives reveal about your dominant worldview?

Keep in mind that you'll return to both of these stories over the course of this book, each time seeing these situations anew, so hold onto your timeline and reflections. Get ready to go deeper. Seeing your own dominant worldview is just the first step in seeing the very different dominant worldviews of the other people who will round out your innovation team.

CHAPTER 2

What Is the Innovation Code?

There is something indulgent—even sinful—about taking a personality test. Whether you're curling up on the couch to take a *Cosmo* quiz about what kind of lover you are or sitting down at your laptop to complete the full 222-question Myers-Briggs questionnaire, you're turning away, if only for a brief moment, from the rest of the world to find out a little bit about yourself. Personality tests appeal to our desire for self-knowledge, but they also tap into our inner narcissists. That's why they're so undeniably, hypnotically, and addictively fun: there's something weirdly rewarding about recognizing ourselves in categories.

That's also why they're often limiting: because they only reveal things about ourselves (and things we usually already know) and not anything about the other people around us. The reality is that we exist in relation to other people, and so, if we want a full understanding of how we function in our worlds, we need to learn things about everyone else—from the people we love most to the people we clash with.

How can a personality test tell us about other people? We might try taking these exams from perspectives outside of our own to get into diverse mindsets that might unsettle and broaden our own thinking. Yet this sounds oxymoronic: a personality test about everyone else but us. We do, after all, have to keep ourselves in the picture.

A Relational
Personality Test

The solution is not a selfless personality test but a relational one—one that indicates types *in relation* to other types, showing how they interact and define each other rather than exist as fixed points on a scale of unchanging identity.

This is where the Innovation Code comes in. The Innovation Code is a sense-making tool to identify, differentiate, and categorize the dominant worldviews we use to approach innovation. Each of these dominant worldviews is unique and important on its own. But it is their interactions that produce meaningful innovation. The Innovation Code spells out the steps to harness the energy that emerges not from the harmony, but from the conflicts between these dominant worldviews to create sustainable innovation practices.

There are four different ways of thinking that push and pull against each other: the Artist, the Engineer, the Sage, and the Athlete. These are dynamic dominant worldviews that do not exist in a vacuum but define themselves in relation to their counterparts. The paradox of growth and innovation is that they are born from the tension and constructive conflict of these opposing personalities and methodologies.

As a framework for identifying your own dominant worldview, the Innovation Code also provides the tools for understanding everyone else, for seeing the other kinds of personalities and approaches that you need to surround yourself with. While typical personality tests claim to tell us who we as individuals are as they classify people in rigid groups, the Innovation Code is a living system that takes into account ever-changing interpersonal dynamics. It tells you not just who you are, but also who you're *not,* who your allies and counterparts are, what brings you all together, and, most importantly, what keeps you all apart.

The Artist vs. the Engineer

The Artist embraces revolutionary growth through wild experimentation and an extreme rejection of conventions. These radical explorers are drawn to breakthrough innovation projects. They create grand visions and are likely to try unexpected solutions. Their core competency is imagination. John Belushi, Coco Chanel, Duke Ellington, and Walt Disney all embody the Artist worldview as their deeply original, even whimsical or offbeat projects come out of the desire for something totally new. While this approach provides the greatest magnitude of growth, it also brings the greatest risk.

At the opposite end of the innovation spectrum from the Artist is the Engineer. These are individuals who seek efficiency and quality and who depend on processes. They are highly disciplined and see the value of systems and bureaucracy. Marie Curie, Emily Post, Carl Sagan, and Sam Walton (founder of Walmart) are all classic Engineers who developed streamlined procedures that could be replicated and reapplied widely. Although the Engineer's approach minimizes the possibility of failure, this methodical march of progress often also brings with it unwanted bureaucracy.

The fundamental difference between the Artist and the Engineer is in the magnitude of innovation. The risky Artist wants breakthrough innovation that can disrupt the way we think and live. The reliable Engineer prefers to tinker with the current system and continuously improve every aspect. Despite—or, really, because of—their contradictory outlooks, those who have an Engineer's attitude and those who identify with the Artist worldview make a wonderful pair, complementing extreme creativity with the reliability of process.

The Sage vs.
the Athlete

Those who have the Sage dominant worldview seek out connection, harmony, and togetherness. They are mentors, facilitators, and team-builders who work with a set of shared values. Their core competency is empathy as they listen carefully and thoughtfully to others, gaining a deep understanding of their peers' desires and needs. Florence Nightingale, Dr. Martin Luther King Jr., Oprah Winfrey, and Jostein Solheim (CEO of Ben & Jerry's) all exemplify this dominant worldview. Their ability to connect with and influence other people is a testament to their remarkable capacity to empathize with them. The Sage is typically associated with the slowest forms of growth because this approach focuses on building the underlying organizational culture and competencies required to sustain it. But the upside of this slowness is its long-term stability: once you establish a sense of community, it can last for many generations.

The Athlete, which is the opposite of the Sage, represents a Darwinist approach that focuses on competition where the strong prevail at the expense of the weak. These kinds of people are often results-driven workhorses. While Sages slowly and patiently build a community and connect with others, Athletes produce profit and speed. They set concrete goals for themselves and meet those goals. Their core competency is courage. Katherine Hepburn, Angela Merkel, Martha Stewart, and Jack Welch (former CEO of General Electric) all epitomize the Athlete's worldview. This form of growth is the fastest of all four, but is not typically sustainable because its "sweatshop" approach shows little concern for the development of others.

The Athlete and the Sage are opposites in the speed in which they innovate. The Athlete understands that time is essential for innovation. Innovation can go sour like milk. Innovative products from last year are no longer on the Christmas list this year. They know they need to commercialize ideas as fast as they can. On the other hand, the Sage understands that the only way to sustainable innovation is to build a deep competency to innovate, which is through developing the innovation culture and practices inside the organization. For all of their apparent differences, the Athlete and the Sage can work well together, combining the long-term focus on values and culture with the short-term emphasis on tangible outcomes.

Table 1, shown below, deciphers how the four dominant worldviews hold distinctive values and approach the world through different perspectives.

The Innovation Code

	ARTIST	ENGINEER	SAGE	ATHLETE
GIFT	Imagination	Discipline	Empathy	Courage
CENTRAL QUESTION	Is it WOW?	Is it functional?	Is it ethical?	Is it valuable?
WHAT THEY SEEK	Transcendence	Perfection	Harmony	Power
HOW THEY SEEK IT	Experimentation	Observation	Reflection	Challenge
WHAT THEY VALUE	Novelty	Standards	Integrity	Winning
HOW THEY CREATE	Vision	Process	Values	Goals

TABLE 1. **FOUR DOMINANT WORLDVIEWS**

In addition to representing different kinds of individuals, each of the four dominant worldviews also represents different kinds of organizational identities. That is, each corresponds to a larger group dynamic. Table 2 below shows how each dominant world-view functions in the individual and organizational levels.

The Self is, of course, much more complicated than a mere personality type. We are a combination of everything. But, despite our quirks and idiosyncrasies, our surprising depths and funny inconsistencies, we all do have an underlying dominant worldview that likely fits one of the four identities.

The challenge is in both embracing and overcoming that dominant worldview. We need to make use of our strengths but also be aware of our shortcomings and surround ourselves with

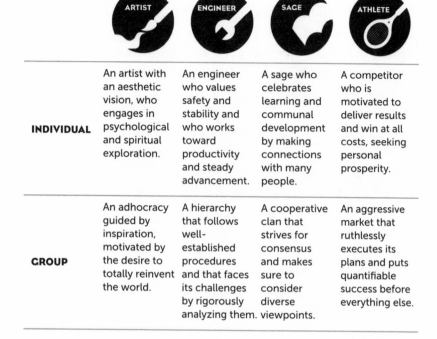

	ARTIST	ENGINEER	SAGE	ATHLETE
INDIVIDUAL	An artist with an aesthetic vision, who engages in psychological and spiritual exploration.	An engineer who values safety and stability and who works toward productivity and steady advancement.	A sage who celebrates learning and communal development by making connections with many people.	A competitor who is motivated to deliver results and win at all costs, seeking personal prosperity.
GROUP	An adhocracy guided by inspiration, motivated by the desire to totally reinvent the world.	A hierarchy that follows well-established procedures and that faces its challenges by rigorously analyzing them.	A cooperative clan that strives for consensus and makes sure to consider diverse viewpoints.	An aggressive market that ruthlessly executes its plans and puts quantifiable success before everything else.

TABLE 2. **INDIVIDUAL AND ORGANIZATIONAL LEVELS**

people who approach things differently than we do. It's comfortable and easy to stick with the things we believe, but by doing so we're also stifling our ability to be innovative. To know the Self is to know other people's selves, too.

Example:
The Dreamer
Meets the Martinet

Consider the story of Sanne. In her youth in the Netherlands, Sanne was a wildly imaginative and artistic girl. She liked to paint colorful and unwieldy murals on the walls of her garage, write fantasy stories in her journals, and perform overly dramatic plays with heroic acts of derring-do for friends and family. It was no surprise that Sanne went on to be a highly successful video game designer, creating imaginative worlds of vibrant characters. Her small boutique company was a mélange of free spirits, eccentrics, and assorted misfits.

While most of their games enjoyed a cult following, one of them became an enormous hit. This brought Sanne's small company to the attention of a number of very large corporations looking for the next big thing. A leading Japanese gaming company offered Sanne an enormous amount of money to acquire her firm with the condition that Sanne stayed on for the next three years to oversee the design and development of a wide array of new video games. Never one to shy away from a challenge, Sanne agreed to the deal and moved her family, as well as some key members of her staff, to the corporation's game design facility in San Diego.

Sanne reported directly to the Chief Technology Officer, Franklin, who had worked in the military sector for 25 years before joining the gaming giant. Much more professional than he was personable, Franklin based his objective judgments on data. A few years away from retirement, he was frustrated that the company had just acquired yet another small boutique software firm without consulting him. The small firms were notorious for using unconventional software languages and design techniques. In Franklin's eyes, integrating the new games of these idiosyncratic firms into the existing technology platform of his streamlined organization was deeply difficult—a nuisance and a disruption. Franklin wished that these smaller companies understood the difference between designing a game for a niche market and developing one that works perfectly every time within the rigid industry standards for the gaming consoles, computers, and smartphones that most people use.

Sanne knew that working in a larger firm would be challenging. What she didn't anticipate was just how much the firm's creative decisions were based more on corporate hierarchy than the desire to produce imaginative products. Yet even though she was unfamiliar and uncomfortable with the firm's elaborate organizational structure and complex processes, Sanne found her new coworkers highly skilled, deeply committed, and generally interesting. She was even more amazed at how well they synchronized all the resources at their disposal to get a game into production and ultimately to the gaming market. This large company deeply understood how to take an idea and get it to scale.

Uncomfortable with her new situation, but optimistic, Sanne proposed an off-site meeting with Franklin's senior staff and her own to see if there was a way to create highly unique games using a standardized process. Franklin reluctantly agreed.

The first meeting didn't go well. They could barely agree on a location, let alone a shared goal or approach to software development. Key members of Sanne's original staff were so frustrated that they resigned and cashed out. Two senior leaders from Franklin's team became passive-aggressive and made it impossible to book the next meeting on their schedules.

But Sanne and Franklin decided to try to meet again. This time, they asked both teams to create a metaphor for the entire software development process. The exercise seemed silly to many of the participants. Nevertheless, they did their best to find a suitable analogy for their combined work: an aquarium, a beehive, and a NASCAR race, just to name a few.

Finally, they stumbled upon the metaphor of a vegetable garden. The combined teams then went into a detailed description of a productive garden. This step was promising, but they wanted to take it even further. For the next meeting, they invited an artist to come and paint a picture of their ideal garden. The artist created a sumptuous scene with bright red peppers reaching for the yellow sun, well-watered rich soil, and honeybees drifting above. Sensing that Franklin was getting a little impatient with the whole shared vision "painting thing," Sanne asked him to translate the picture back into his own operation. Franklin didn't understand what she meant. But some members of his team gave it a try: the water was the unseen and underlying process necessary for all sustainable software development, a swarm of bees were marketing spreading pollen from one plant to the next, the vegetables were the delicious games, and the sun represented customers, for without their nurturing energy, nothing grows. The more they translated the painting into the operational details of the design and development process, the clearer it became how the design of the game and its development and distribution were all interrelated.

Franklin then asked the combined teams to describe the current state of their garden and asked the painter to paint it: dry soil in need of water, a single bee buzzing above, shriveled and undersized vegetables, and the setting sun. Now they had two paintings—one of a beautiful garden and one in need of attention. In the two images, the team saw both the solution and the problem. They continued to work through the metaphor of how to transform their current garden into their desired garden. Vision and process were finally integrated. Roles and responsibilities became clear, and tasks were assigned.

Sanne, the Artist, and Franklin, the Engineer, soon realized that they could help each other succeed. They still frequently disagreed but worked together to find hybrid solutions. Sanne would bring imaginative ideas to Franklin and ask for his thoughts on how to make it work. Sometimes Sanne would have to limit the uniqueness of her design, while other times Franklin would have to incorporate a new technique into his standardized development process. Over time, the two became a dynamic team. Franklin eventually retired and Sanne became the CEO of the company, which prospers to this very day.

In the end, what both Franklin and Sanne understood beautifully was their own messiness—their own flaws and shortcomings. It was this great self-insight that allowed them to accept the necessity of their seeming opponents. They had the potential to become rivals, but instead they became collaborators. This isn't to say that they got along. In fact, their clashing was the very energy that made their joint efforts so successful. In the next chapter, we'll look more deeply at how and when conflict becomes constructive and why that conflict is actually the best way to produce something entirely new.

Summary

The Innovation Code presents four dominant worldviews—the main opposing approaches to growth and creativity: the Artist, the Engineer, the Sage, and the Athlete. For all our individual complexity, we all have one overpowering identity. Innovating is about understanding the gifts of that identity but also about seeing its shortcomings so we can seek out the people who will make up for those shortcomings.

Exercise

Let's find your dominant worldview. Ask yourself the following questions. If you are unsure, think about what you would do under pressure. Usually our true selves emerge when we are under pressure or in crisis. You can also take the assessment online. Please refer to The Innovation Code Supplemental Material section on page 129.

1. What is the most important thing to you?

A. Doing things first
B. Doing things fast
C. Doing things right
D. Doing things together

2. What are you the best at?

A. Starting something new
B. Defeating obstacles
C. Improving how things work
D. Building relationships

3. How would you best describe yourself?

A. Creative
B. Decisive
C. Organized
D. Caring

4. How do you make decisions?

A. I brainstorm through all possible options
B. I start with the results I want and work backwards to what I need to do

C. I follow precedents and a set of rules and norms

D. I work to get consensus

5. What do you invest your time in?

A. New ideas

B. Winning projects and ventures

C. Systems and technology

D. High-potential people

6. What do you do the most as a leader?

A. I anticipate future trends

B. I make firm decisions

C. I use systems to make things run more efficiently

D. I listen to others

7. What is the role that you most relate to?

A. I create new products

B. I solve problems as soon as they occur

C. I cut back on mistakes

D. I solve conflicts

8. How are you best described in your daily life?

A. Inspiring

B. Self-reliant

C. Disciplined

D. Sociable

9. What attribute applies to you the most?

A. Curious

B. Direct

C. Precise

D. Kind

For each answer, place a number 1 in the corresponding cell in Table 3 below. Add up the rows to create totals for A, B, C, and D. For example, if you choose answer B in Question 1, enter a 1 in the column B.

QUESTION	A	B	C	D
1				
2				
3				
4				
5				
6				
7				
8				
9				
TOTAL				

TABLE 3. **ASSESSMENT**

Add the entries in each column. The column with the highest total represents your dominant worldview. If the A column has the highest total, you are an Artist. If B, you are an Athlete; if C, an Engineer; and if D, a Sage.

CHAPTER 3

Constructive Conflict

The Innovation Code is an argument waiting to happen. Put an Artist, an Athlete, a Sage, and an Engineer in one room, and give them a problem to solve; things will get messy. When four intensely different—and in many ways opposing—viewpoints come together, conflict is a given. But conflict doesn't have to be a bad thing. In fact, conflict is the very force that will bring about the best outcome in almost any given innovation initiative. The only way to create unlikely yet groundbreaking, provocative, and winning solutions is to build a team that doesn't agree—a team that challenges each other by combining deeply dissimilar worldviews.

The Innovation Code is less like fission—the separation of a heavy, unstable atom into two smaller ones—and more like fusion, the merging of two different atoms into a bigger one. It's no coincidence that fusion produces so much more energy than fission that it's enough to power the sun: bringing together instability is more powerful than breaking it apart. Just consider the example of Devi.

Example:
The Doctor Who Hated Procedures

Devi was a doctor who hated procedures. She'd gone into medicine to discover something new—not repeat the things that every other medical professional had done before her. A practitioner with the experimental ambitions of an inventor, sometimes even an artist, Devi was the most creative physician in her class all through medical school. Although she went to a prestigious university and was schooled in the most advanced surgical techniques and cutting-edge drug therapies, she traveled the world to learn about alternative treatments from midwives and medicine men.

In her residency, Devi stirred the pot. The attending physician who supervised her wasn't impressed or amused by her adventuresome approach to the healing arts. He called her out when he thought her treatment plans were too unconventional, and she fired right back with brilliant justifications for her nonstandard strategies.

The back and forth made things perpetually tense. Devi almost always had to follow the orders of the attending doctor. Quietly seething, she got through her residency with the knowledge that she'd one day get to do things her own way. Her superior constantly advised her to be more accepting of the status quo, but he never totally silenced her: he admired her superb diagnostic skills and her excellent bedside manner.

At the end of her residency, Devi couldn't be more hopeful for the future. Filled with high ideals and enthusiasm that she could introduce new approaches to traditional Western medicine, Devi went to work as a general practitioner in a holistic physician's practice group. At first, it was fantastic. There were few policies and procedures and little bureaucracy to get in the way of attending to patients. Devi and her colleagues saw little need for appointments, scheduling, or lengthy legal forms. She worked arduously to create a medical practice that treated the whole patient.

Devi dreamed of an office that felt more like a comfortable home than a series of waiting rooms. So she and her colleagues reinvested most of the money they made into the purchase of a lovely old manor house and moved all of the staff across town to the historic district. With every year came new ventures: a homeopathic pharmacy, a neuromuscular therapy clinic, and acupuncture services. Devi's creative ventures had worked so well that they made her the managing physician.

There was just one problem—and it was a big one: Devi wasn't a manager. The medical practice had grown so large that Devi couldn't run it effectively. Scheduling snafus and insurance errors abounded. And since each doctor practiced their own form of alternative medicine, cost overruns left the practice unexpectedly strapped for cash. Meeting after meeting, Devi tried to get the doctors to make decisions, but their shared stubbornness and divergent ideas for improvement left the doctors in a deadlock. Devi knew she had to step up and take action to save the practice.

With a disconcerting sense of déjà vu, Devi realized that she had to seek out the very things she had worked so hard to avoid: policies, procedures, and bureaucratic systems. She had to hire the types of people she'd always been most uncomfortable around: financial officers, systems operators, and lawyers. Her new recruits asked her to invest in an integrated array of technologies and accounting systems. It took a while to get used to all of the rules and to get over her fundamental aversion to rules themselves, but eventually Devi came to admire and depend on the professionals she had nothing in common with. She saw that they made it possible for her to do what she did best—heal patients.

Devi is an unwitting testament to the underestimated, often misunderstood power of constructive conflict. It's a statement we've all heard, but it's never more true than when it comes to innovation: too much of the same thing isn't good. A medical practice full of Devis—Artists—is, in the long run, dysfunctional. A medical practice full of doctors like the attending physician she couldn't stand—Engineers—is, in the long run, *too* functional, slick and smooth at the expense of new ideas and approaches.

Devi's story turns us back to the paradox of dominant worldviews that started this book: because our dominant worldviews influence the way we see everything, we need to work with people who have different dominant worldviews than our own, to add nuance, thoughtfulness, and surprise insights to our own perspectives. It's not about avoiding extremes—it's about putting extremes together and generating something productive from the way they clash.

Two Forms of
Constructive Conflict

There are two major kinds of constructive conflict that propel innovation at the personal and organizational level: the disharmony between Artists and Engineers (as evidenced by Devi's story) and the tension between Sages and Athletes.

The two struggles correspond to the two different dynamics of innovation: magnitude and speed. When it comes to the magnitude—or the intensity—of an innovation, Artists drive Engineers to be more radical while Engineers rein in Artists, bringing some pragmatism to their visions. When it comes to the speed of an innovation, Sages slow Athletes down, encouraging them to build a culture that will last for generations, while Athletes keep the Sage's head in the game, calling attention to quick wins and short-term strategy.

While these two forms of conflict are the fundamental dissonances that propel innovation and growth, it's crucial that all four of the dominant worldviews interact with each other. The ideal team or organization contains Sages, Artists, Engineers, *and* Athletes. The key is not to strike a balance but to know when you need more or less of each approach.

The Developmental Phases of Growth
From Artist to Athlete to Sage to Engineer

The need for each approach depends on where your team or organization is in the developmental phases of growth. At their onset, groups need more Artists and Athletes. Artists will give a young company a creative edge, while Athletes come up with a playbook, a way of getting finances and resources together to prevent the Artists' great ideas from imploding. With Artists and Athletes working together—two externally-facing forms of innovation, looking for new markets and technologies—the organization begins to grow very fast. This is called the sigmoid "S." Organizations don't grow in nice, smooth lines—they grow ballistically (Figure 1).

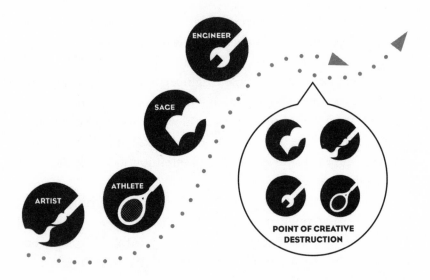

FIGURE 1. **ORGANIZATIONAL GROWTH CYCLE**

As it starts to grow, the organization has to get the right people and community involved and develop the best customer relationships. This is when the company needs Sages. Finally, when the organization gets really big, it needs structure, processes, and hierarchy—the gifts of Engineers.

At the Point of
Creative Destruction

When an organization matures, it typically stalls. This is called flatlining. The sigmoid "S" suddenly starts to decelerate. This is where most organizations die—at the point of creative destruction. At this moment, the organization needs to find a way to reinvent itself. The company must overcome its dominant worldview and identify the form of innovation that it needs more of. Instead of maintaining the same ratio of different kinds of thinkers, the organization needs to incorporate more Artists or Athletes or Sages or Engineers, whichever form will add more variance to the current situation.

The key is in knowing where to look for the right people to recruit and how to recruit them. Seek out people with extensive experience in their fields. Experience can come in many forms—from the theoretical knowledge of a researcher to the practical mastery of an engineer. Remember that experience does not necessarily mean age. In fact, if you were building a project around an emerging trend or a new market, youth would be an asset on your team.

The goal is to assemble a diversity of perspectives and expertise. Recruit individuals who have different visions of your company—some who see it as a radical organization moving toward the future, others who see it as a highly efficient operational machine, and yet others who see its internal culture.

Where to Find Your
Future Collaborators

Look in both likely and unlikely places for your future collaborators. They might be inside your organization—but they might also be elsewhere, out in the real world. Everyone is a superhero in some context—and inept in a different context. A Harvard PhD candidate in Medieval History who's recently become a mother could benefit from talking to a stay-at-home father of five children. That same father, who wants to finish his novel-in-progress, could benefit from talking to the PhD candidate's good friends who work in publishing.

Every kind of thinker has a different way of speaking—and when we approach people who aren't like us, we need to adapt to their mode of communication. We need to speak their language. Appeal to their values and interests and present questions and projects in their terms.

Artists engage in experiments and express themselves in creative outlets, so be enthusiastic and energetic when talking to them. Ask open-ended questions. Stress the radical potential and possibility of new solutions that comes with your project.

Engineers share data, so give them statistics and concrete information when describing your project to them. Offer them a sense of the step-by-step process behind your initiative. Provide details and explain things in a sequential order.

Athletes get to the point, so frame your initiative to them as a win-or-lose situation with a concrete payoff. Use quantifiable facts to illustrate your point. Show the logical necessity of your project.

Sages gather together and talk about their feelings, so take your time and get to know them on a personal level. Put them at ease and talk about life experiences. Establish a sense of community when asking them to join your team.

An Inside-Out
Perspective on Innovation

As an innovation leader, you will find it important to take an inside-out perspective in developing your team. First, look at your own skills and decide objectively where you think you might be incompetent. Give those kinds of tasks and responsibilities to another member of your team. Next, look at the areas where you are merely competent and assign these actions to other members of your team to supplement your own competency. Then, find the areas where you are masterful and choose a member of your team whom you can train as your understudy in those tasks. Finally, determine the areas in which you are unique—your one-of-a-kind gifts or skills. Here is the part of the innovation leadership proposition that you need to focus on. This is the way to maximize your own value to the team.

Teams are works in progress. They are dynamic groups that you need to add to and take away from as you move along in your project and see what you need more and less of. The same people who are great at starting a project are not the same people who are great at getting the project to scale.

Conflict is inevitable when you put such a wide variety of perspectives on one team—and that's a good thing. The ugliest word in innovation is apathy. When an Engineer clashes with an Artist or an Athlete butts heads with a Sage, resist your impulse to bring about peace. Engage. Dwell in the conflict. See what happens when opponents push each other to their limits. For that is when the game-changing hybrid solutions you never could've foreseen on your own arise. The best hybrid solution is a temporary one. In solving the immediate conflict, it sets the stage for the next better conflict. Like a boxing match with infinite rounds of ever-escalating intensity, innovation is a year-round sport.

Summary

The two main forms of conflict are the ones between Artists and Engineers (over the size of innovation) and between Sages and Athletes (over the speed of innovation). At different moments in the life cycle of an innovation initiative, different dominant worldviews must come out on top: Artists and Athletes are great at launching an innovation while Sages and Engineers can establish the long-term environment for sustaining an innovation.

Exercise

Return to the two stories you told about yourself at the end of the first chapter—the story of failure and the story of success. Now, instead of focusing on what you did, reflect on what the people around you did.

Consider three competing (and complementing) levels:

1. Think about the largest level—the setting: Where were you? At college? In your company? Around your family? At home? Characterize the larger space of your surroundings and consider the external factors at play.

2. Then, think about the second-largest level—the characters: Who else was involved? Your friends? Colleagues? Strangers? Parents? Children? How did these other people influence the outcome of the situation?

3. Finally, think about the smallest level—yourself. You've already considered yourself in the Chapter One exercise, but now that you've considered all these other people and factors, return to those questions of self. How did the setting and characters affect your own thoughts, actions, and decisions? How does understanding this change the way you think about the larger dynamics of your life? How can you better welcome constructive conflict into your life?

CHAPTER 4

Dwelling in the Conflict

Behind some of the twentieth century's most iconic love songs is a series of prolonged, tense, irreconcilable conflicts. In the writing room and the recording studio, John Lennon and Paul McCartney were everything their music wasn't: disharmonious, discordant, hostile. As professional partners, their worldviews couldn't have been more different. Lennon, the Artist, was the nonconformist, always looking for the next big thing. McCartney, the Engineer, sought beauty by embracing order. Far from putting their differences aside, the diametrically opposed geniuses dwelled in the conflict. They didn't fake accord for the sake of a peaceful working relationship. They were competitive with one another and pushed and pulled each other as they cowrote albums that managed to alternately highlight their divergent gifts. They didn't compromise. They didn't give in to the other. They elevated each other through their conflict. In seven years of constructive conflict, they wrote close to 200 songs and released 13 albums. The two men who made irresistible, genre-defining art out of the simple wish to hold your lover's hand might've, under all other circumstances, very well preferred to be apart from each other.

This kind of constructive conflict is crucial in any creation process—not just for the collaborative production of art but for any degree of innovation in your life or your organization. And you don't need to be a once- (or twice-) in-a-millennium virtuoso to cultivate constructive conflict.

In fact, there are concrete steps you can take to generate positive deviance in your innovation initiative. This isn't to say that they're easy and always guaranteed to work. Quite the contrary: this is a complicated process that takes long periods of practice and failing to finally find success. Like playing a piano, dwelling in conflict is a skill you need to try and try doing over again to perfect. And, in the process, it will take you to uncomfortable places. But that's a discomfort—like the conflict itself—that you can and should dwell in. The very impulse to innovate comes from a negative feeling, a form of dissatisfaction: you're unhappy with the present and so you want to make it better and new. Harness that dissatisfaction and make it into productive energy. As you work through that dissatisfaction, the discomfort will get greater before it lessens; the mess will get bigger before it becomes manageable. Don't try to tidily clean up the mess. Get deeper in it and follow these steps:

1. Assemble a diversity of perspectives

2. Engage in the conflict

3. Establish a shared goal or vision

4. Construct hybrid solutions

Step 1:
Assemble a Diversity of Perspectives

You won't solve your grand innovation problem by simply thinking about it on your own on the way to work or in the shower. Innovation is fundamentally dialogical in nature: it is born out of conversations with other people who may feed off of, enhance, challenge, push back against, nurture, or even totally reject our own ideas or solutions. These conversations are a form of discovery, a way of exploring new possibilities. These exploratory conversations are the early part of any innovation.

But even before you have these conversations, you need to know who to have these conversations with. Begin by taking a good and honest look at yourself—not who you want to be, but who you are now. What are you good at? What are you bad at? How do you normally approach a problem? What kind of an innovator are you? Then you need to gather people who are not like you. The ideal is to find people from all four kinds of dominant worldviews. These people don't need to get along. You don't need them to agree. Ideally, they *won't* agree and will own their disagreement. Seek out people who aren't afraid to speak their mind and who won't back down from their differing opinions.

If you can't find people from all four dominant worldviews—or if you're trying to solve a problem on your own—you can engage in some imaginative and experimental thinking outside of your own biases. Envision a board of directors. Populate that hypothetical board of directors with people you associate with each of the four dominant worldviews, people you personally know, or outspoken public personalities who fit any given type. Ask yourself questions from the perspective of these people. How would a Sage approach this problem? What solutions would an Athlete come up with? For every viewpoint's suggested strategy, generate a list of five strengths and weaknesses that you can then share and discuss with your chosen interlocutors.

Make Conflict Normative

The idea here is to create as many different opportunities as possible. This is something you should do all of the time and for every situation. The goal is to assemble a group of interlocutors you can consult regularly, to create a long-term, sustainable culture out of constructive conflict. Positive deviance should be part of everyday life, of doing business as usual. Conflict must become normative. In all other situations, it's our impulse to resolve or eliminate conflict. In the world of innovation, though, we need to resist that impulse, resist alignment. Make conflict a healthy, generative element of your day-to-day functioning. Consider building a network of creativity clusters or an innovation hub—or some kind of incentive for dynamic dialogues. It's important that these conversations happen in open and safe spaces where people feel empowered and unencumbered when they come together and talk through complicated issues. You might find a space outside of your office and headquarters, where everyone is on even ground, a neutral zone—an innovation Switzerland.

Take, for example, the story of a struggling symphony orchestra that needed the freshness of constructive conflict to launch the innovative mindset that would save its life. Symphonies across the country are facing a crisis. Symphony attendance by those under forty has plummeted over the past decade at an alarming rate. Yet endowments by patrons over forty have remained relatively steadfast over the same period. This support keeps an increasingly aged audience in orchestra hall seats at the expense of developing programming that will attract the next generation of symphony goers. So the very people who hope to perpetuate the love of symphonic music are actually unwittingly creating a barrier to that possibility. The challenge orchestras face is not to invent something new but to develop a new solution to bring their enduring gifts into new environments.

One symphony in particular met this challenge by facilitating positive deviance. The first step was jumpstarting conversations between people with different perspectives who wouldn't have otherwise come together—and who inevitably (but productively) clashed. This involved gathering people both inside and well beyond the orchestra, from engineers, business experts, and design gurus to undergraduate students, professors, and industry professionals, many of whom had no direct investment in the orchestra itself. Rather, it was their outside expertise and experience that the orchestra hoped would spark attention toward the new solutions it needed to attract new listeners and patrons. These unlikely teams, not of friends and colleagues but of strangers and outsiders, were the start of the dialogues that launched real innovation.

Step 2:
Engage in the Conflict

Like is a four-letter word in the world of innovation. Think of innovation as the opposite of social media: whereas social media is about liking and sharing posts we agree with and building a collection—really, a bubble—of people we're friends with, innovation is about reaching outside of our immediate circles. This doesn't mean that you should dislike and disagree with your interlocutors just to create conflict. It just means that you should feel invested in voicing meaningful dissent.

In the case of the diverse teams of outsiders working to brainstorm ways to save the struggling symphony orchestra, meaningful dissent came in the form of fiery breakout dialogues. Naturally, the industry professionals didn't agree with the undergraduate students. The design gurus clashed with the professors. To keep the disagreements civil, no one ever called an idea ridiculous or irrelevant. Instead, they wrote even the most ridiculous ideas down and remained open-minded.

Meaningful dissent comes from a shared investment in your project. For all their encouraged disagreement, team members should be on the same page when it comes to their goals and enthusiasm for the initiative. So, conflict doesn't equal war. It's not about being right or destroying the other side. It's about understanding everyone's point of view and using the multiplicity of viewpoints to create a hybrid solution—one that you couldn't have come up with on your own and one that takes you to a higher place than any individual solution. Use the conflict to raise your project to another level.

Constructive conflict is conflict with empathy. Empathy is not something we usually bring to an argument. Normally, when you're arguing with someone, you want to make sure your opinion comes out on top. In the open space of innovation, generative arguing entails understanding where the other person is coming from and seeing the value of that perspective. Imagine experiencing the world like they do and see the insights that those experiences might give you. Experience, feel, understand—be patient and open-minded.

Doing this takes courage. That's because simply listening to opposing views is hearing criticism of your own. Even more daunting is the conscious cultivation of empathy. For putting yourself in other people's situations may change—even destroy—your own worldview completely. But that's the way we grow and innovate. Growth requires pain.

When brainstorming, communing, conversing—and arguing—make sure to give each participant the same amount of opportunity, regardless of his or her job title. All interlocutors need to be able to voice their ideas. Try using a communal white board and making everyone write on the board. Don't assign a scribe. The scribe is always inevitably either the least powerful or most powerful person in the room.

It's often easiest to recruit a third-party facilitator who can manage these fiery discussions. Outside Sages or Athletes can make the best team managers. As managers, Sages are great at eliciting participation, diffusing disagreements, and finding consensus. This is what Brian Epstein did for the Beatles, mediating their most intense and destructive inner disputes. As managers, Athletes act quite differently. They keep the team on track by focusing on goals, milestones, and timelines. That's what George Martin did every time he reminded the Beatles that they only had so many hours to record their songs.

Step 3:
Establish a Shared
Goal or Vision

What is the problem you're trying to solve? This is a deceptively easy question. On the surface, it seems obvious. Yet the reality is that often people on the same team have different ideas of what their actual project is—especially when they come from such dramatically different viewpoints. The other thing is that often the problem itself changes through the course of its development.

Asking yourself and your teammates to describe the problem at each stage of its planning and execution is important at a practical level. If everyone can reach a common understanding of the problem, the team will avoid getting stuck arguing over ideology. At a more fundamental level, it also can be a shared motivator. The shared goal or vision can be the thing that inspires people to work through the conflict.

If you cannot agree on the initial problem or if the shared vision is not inspiring enough, dig deeper at the root cause. What is actually the root of the problem? Consider a tier-one automobile supplier company that thought it had a wiring manufacturing issue. It wasn't until after some deeper questioning that the team members realized the actual issue was one of connectivity, that the real pressing matter was to make cars lighter and smaller. Discovering your problem is sometimes the hardest part of solving it.

The jumpstart teams behind the symphony orchestra's innovation initiative reached surprising shared goals that dramatically shaped the direction of their future. Symphony leaders learned about how technology has been changing the delivery of musical content, why exactly the music hall has become almost irrelevant, and started to understand that patrons of the arts no longer need go to the music hall to achieve the symphony experience. They began to see that arts patrons are looking to connect more collaboratively with artists on their own time and that the current potential customers pool reveal much younger, diverse, and technologically savvy groups, who want a different type of musical experience: customized, in their own time, and accessible. This is the game-changing insight that inspired the orchestra to reinvent its outreach approaches.

Step 4:
Construct Hybrid Solutions

The point of constructive conflict is to create solutions that you'd never be able to come up with on your own. The key to surprise solutions is hybridity—putting together two ideas or approaches to create a greater one. This is exactly what the symphony orchestra did in its self-reinvention project. Symphony leaders combined the fresh insights and perspectives of outsiders with their own traditions to birth new outreach strategies, from orchestral flash mobs in IKEA to a new smaller performance space devoted to outreach concerts to live webcasts and technological interactions with fans.

To construct hybrid solutions, you need to start by finding two great ideas that are very different and then force fitting them together. This may feel awkward at first, because things don't seem right together. But as you get better at this, this step will become more and more natural to you. Often, creating a metaphor or analogy will help. Once you have an analogy, work backwards to flush out the details of the hybrid idea. Remember the story of Sanne and Franklin? They use the image of planting a vegetable garden to bridge their differences and create something together. Your analogy or metaphor can be anything as long as it is relevant and makes sense to everyone in the team.

Hybrid solutions take initiatives to the next level because they combine the best forces of individual brilliance. Don't settle for what geniuses can do alone. Strive for what different kinds of experts can discover when working with (and pushing against) each other.

Innovation Happens in Phases

Start with Lennon, end with McCartney. Innovation happens in phases, and at every moment, one viewpoint is more important than the other. No one can be fully effective at all phases of innovation. It's crucial that you understand when each worldview should be put first.

In the beginning, the Artist is likely to be the most important contributor. Her divergent point of view looks to the future and opens new possibilities. This is the moment when the Engineer should contribute least, as she's likely to eliminate the *wow* factor of an innovation because her mind always goes to practical concerns, asking what's actually possible. At the tail end of an innovation, when you need to bring the project to scale, the Engineer steps in as the driving force as her expertise with process and reliability becomes most important, and her talent for tinkering and improving things is vital. By this point, an Artist will likely have lost interest and be searching for the next avant-garde thing.

In the middle stages, Sages and Athletes are invaluable. A Sage negotiates, gets buy-in, and pushes the innovation through the organization, while an Athlete keeps the project on track, hits all the success measures, and grows momentum. These two need each other. Without the Athlete, the Sage is too busy bringing everyone along to hit important milestones. Without the Sage, the Athlete plows through without any buy-in or support.

One of the most important things about leading and managing innovation is keeping the team flexible and realizing when the current team configuration no longer produces the constructive conflict you need. Some team members can also burn out or can no longer contribute because of other commitments or assignments. Keep your network wide and platoon players in and out as you need them. Do not be afraid to try different combinations of people. Learn what makes the team work and create some rules that you can use for the future.

All innovations end. There is a natural end to any creative lifecycle. Brian Epstein's death precipitated the breakup of the Beatles. Without the glue that held the band together, the man who helped the guys work through their conflict and maintain their shared vision, the band's demise became inevitable. John became increasingly unsatisfied with the production of his songs and found inspiration in Yoko instead. A true Engineer, Paul wanted to make sure that the band continued to make good financial decisions without Epstein. But when he wanted to bring in a different manager, the others refused. Paul and John could no longer collaborate on songs. The constructive conflict was no longer sustainable.

The next problem and the next agents of constructive conflict that will power its solution: that's the innovation afterlife. The hope is that if you've successfully created a culture of constructive conflict, where positive deviance is an everyday norm and the teams of people who practice it are ever-changing, you're already looking toward the future.

Summary

Practice constructive conflict by moving through four steps: assemble a diversity of perspectives, engage in the conflict, establish a shared goal or vision, and construct hybrid solutions. The challenge is in resisting our normal impulses. Usually when it comes to conflict, we want to eliminate it or avoid it altogether. In the world of innovation, we need to not only dwell in it but also make it a regular part of our lives.

Exercise

In this spirit of making conflict a normal part of the way we function, return to the same stories you examined at the end of Chapter One and Chapter Three. Now that you've considered how all the various internal and external factors came together to influence the either successful or unsuccessful outcome, look for simple rules you can glean from those experiences. Consider overarching patterns of thinking and translate them into guidelines for future behavior. Here are some examples: never enter into a business agreement before working with the other person for at least ninety days; always say yes when a great opportunity presents itself; don't make decisions about important relationships when you're angry.

CHAPTER 5

The Artist

Tom never did anything according to plan. He grew up in a factory town in the middle of Wisconsin dairy country but found small-town America suffocating, even odious. A champion wrestler and the lead player in the high school musical, Tom was at once a jock and a joker. For a young man in his position, the options for the future were anything but limitless: choose between two paths—working on the assembly line or managing the local burger joint, where he frequently hung out. If he were lucky, he might play guitar in a local band or relive his teenage passion by getting involved in the civic theater.

So it was quite a surprise when the guidance counselor called Tom down to his office for a discussion about his prospects. A mediocre student at best, Tom had apparently taken a college admissions test and scored in the top one percent of all Wisconsin high school graduates. After double checking that there wasn't a mix-up or some diabolical deceit at play, the counselor suggested that Tom enroll in the regional campus of the state university because he didn't want to encourage the young man to fly too high too soon.

Tom had other plans. He defiantly announced that, contrary to his apparently auspicious performance on some silly exam, he was going to Broadway to be an actor, director, and playwright. He'd rejected the assembly line and burger joint route, but in a wildly—indeed, *too* wildly—different way than everyone else encouraged.

It took the clear words of his level-headed brother to get Tom to step foot on campus. Once his brother convinced him that, just in case he didn't make it to the top of the theatre world right away, it would be wise to have a degree, Tom visited the university. When the school offered to waive his tuition because of his top test scores, Tom could no longer resist. He enrolled the following semester.

In college, Tom joined the oratorical society and majored in film and theater. Sitting through lectures about the history of the art forms he was fascinated by and having conversations with professors who studied them rigorously made him see that there were many different ways to engage with his passions that didn't only involve creation.

It was in these alternate modes of engagement where Tom actually found himself at his most creative space. His study habits were bizarre. He made giant storyboards to make sense of complex subjects and to see how they connected—not unlike the way a director or novelist might conceptualize a multi-arc narrative. Despite, or more likely *because,* of these quirks, he graduated with honors a year early.

Degree in hand and eager to make the move to New York, Tom once again faced an unlikely alternative option. He was offered a scholarship to attend graduate school and teach public speaking at a top university in California. Unexpectedly intrigued by the prospect of this totally different plan, Tom moved almost 3,000 miles away from the Broadway of his dreams. In less than seven years, Tom had gone from blue-collar trouper to whizz-kid professor. His peculiar way of doing things hadn't changed since high school, but these new places and new people around him embraced his unorthodox approaches. The further up he moved, the more his clever ways of solving problems and presenting ideas were encouraged and valued.

Tom went on to be a leading professor and helped develop an important school of thought along with some other irregulars he had met along the way. At his twenty-fifth high school reunion, a classmate remarked that she always thought that he would go on to be a performer. Tom thought about it for a moment and responded that in fact that's exactly what he had become. Theater became teaching, music became writing, and creativity became new methodology. Every time he delivered a speech, he was the star and director of his own show. In the end, Broadway became the stages of the ivory tower. The iconoclast had found a home he'd seen in none of his former visions of the future.

Artistic Expression
Beyond Artistry

Tom embodies all of the hallmarks of the Artist. His resistance to conformity, outside-of-the-box thinking, tendency to challenge norms, and constant search for something new are the fundamental qualities that make Artists who they are.

The name might sound misleading: Artists are not necessarily actual artists or people who make a living with their creative works, but they do have an elemental creative impulse that drives the way they see and experience their worlds. In many ways, the visionary talent of the Artist is the kind of thinking that people associate most with innovation.

Artists are people who pursue revolutionary breaks from the past and breakthrough ideas. They thrive in situations riddled with uncertainty and doubt—contexts that their peers might avoid—because they are great experimenters. They strive to orient their products, services, and ideas to the future.

What Artists seek is radical innovation. They want organic growth—things not acquired but built. These people are revolutionaries. They are dreamers—expressive, clever, optimistic, charismatic, and quick on their feet.

At the organizational level, the Artistic organization is a company with few rules and many voices. A prophetic vision is what carries an Artistic workplace: stimulating projects, flexible hours, new initiatives, and independent work streams. This is an environment driven by frenetic energy. Think Pixar. Think early Apple and late Apple. Think Vera Wang and Gianni Versace. Think Walt Disney and Steve Jobs. These are game changers. This is the high-risk, high-reward innovation approach.

Don't Leave an
Artist Alone

For everyone who makes it, there are hundreds more who fail. Therein lies the Artist's greatest weakness: the inability to see the concerns of reality. Left alone, the Artist lives a life of total chaos.

Just look at the alternate life of Tom had he not been advised by pragmatic mentors and peers: suddenly, the could've-been whizz-kid professor rejects the education he never knew he needed and becomes the starving Broadway actor with no plan to fall back on. On the one hand, Tom's instincts were always right. He was right to want to leave rural Wisconsin, to see a bigger future for himself. On the other hand, Tom's visions were too wild. His true creative talents weren't in theater acting or filmmaking. Rather, his gifts of speech and narrative were meant for the academic stage. Every Artist needs someone else to help them to first channel their intensely creative energies to the right productive outlets and then to rein in those creative energies according to the relevant task and context.

The key to mastering the art of being and befriending an Artist is to know when you need to be revolutionary and when you need to be conventional.

In the life cycle of a company, it makes sense to embrace Artists at the earliest stage of development—and then again, much later on, when you need to breathe new life into your organization.

Example:
Apple

Take, for example, a company we all know: Apple. In its first stage, Apple was a completely Artistic endeavor, founded in a garage by a group of revolutionary thinkers who wanted to make computers easy enough for everyone to use. It became the darling of the stock exchange. Like-minded free thinkers supported the company and its universal, chic accessibility. Here, it was at the peak of its Artistic sensibility.

As the computer business grew and established industry-wide standards, Apple could no longer retain its Artistic identity. In its second stage, it became an outsider in the very segment that it helped spawn. The PC market has grown by leaps and bounds and overtook Apple's market share. Steve Jobs, cofounder of Apple, was kicked out of the company over constant disagreement with John Sculley, the CEO at the time, on Apple's future. Sculley wanted to move to open architecture and focus on schools and small businesses. Jobs wanted to continue to use the closed architecture model, differentiate the brand, and compete head-to-head with IBM. Without Jobs, Apple became a turnkey operation that produced software and computers that were relatively similar to the rest of the industry.

On the verge of bankruptcy in the late 1990s, Apple returned to its revolutionaries-in-a-garage spirit. Jobs came back and revitalized Apple by reintroducing the radical, visionary thinking it depended on in its infancy. In one of his most controversial moves ever, Jobs turned to the enemy and collaborated with Microsoft to bring Office to Apple users in return for a sizeable investment. With room and time afforded by Microsoft's lifeline, Jobs was able to transform Apple and develop an entire ecosystem of products and software that went beyond the computer—including a music-downloading site and handheld devices.

In this last stage, Apple looks a lot like it did when it was a startup. The reason is this: at both of these moments, the risk of trying something radical and the reward of staying the same were reversed. The only significant difference between the two situations is that now, in this later stage, in addition to being the Artistic company it was at its start, there is also a secondary component to its identity that encourages it to produce replicable and reliable earnings. The best Artist is the one who can turn on and off his or her gifts at the appropriate moments. There is a time and a place for revolutionary thinking.

Exercise:
Scenario Making

Not everyone is an Artist, but there are ways that anyone can become more creative when the moment demands a new way of seeing things. You don't have to wait for an Artist to join your team—or wait for inspiration to miraculously strike—in order to gain the benefits or insights of an Artist. Consider this exercise of scenario-making to see the future first like an Artist.

Artists try to see the future first because they aspire to create new things in new ways. Because there is no data on the future, we can only look for those forces that drive the future in a particular way: money, relationships, employment, health, and so on. It's important that we look only at those drivers that relate to our plans and aspirations. Otherwise, it's easy to get lost in all the complexity.

Scenario making simply means developing a collection of stories about what could happen in the future. This will give us some clues as to what we will see along the way so that we can navigate our way through potential barriers toward our vision. We make scenarios routinely when we consider the best and worst case of a decision. What we are assessing is the relative probability that something will actually happen and the relative impact of it. Follow these steps to see the future:

1. First, list a dozen things that could make or break your vision. Consider the list from the perspectives of all four dominant worldviews.

Examples:

- Artist: fashion trends and breakthrough inventions
- Engineer: government regulations and industry standards
- Athlete: probable competitors and potential investors
- Sage: customer requirements and community needs

Look for blind spots—the areas typically overlooked by your dominant worldview. From each point of view, look for opportunities, challenges, what is truly known, and what we need to find out.

2. Now create a table like the one below (Table 4). The Y-axis represents the impact of the event from low to high, and the X-axis the probability of the event happening from low to high. Assess each item in your list in terms of its relative probability and impact on your vision. Does it have a high impact, and is it highly probable that it will happen? Or is it of low impact, but highly probable? Put each item in the list in the appropriate places in the table. Be careful not to overestimate or underestimate. Try to be as objective and realistic as possible. Once you are done with the list, highlight only those high-probability and/or high-impact forces that drive the future of your vision. There should only be a few of these. Ignore the other forces.

WATCH IT	PLAN ON IT	PLAN ON IT
FORGET IT	WATCH IT	PLAN ON IT
FORGET IT	FORGET IT	WATCH IT

IMPACT

PROBABILITY

TABLE 4. **OPPORTUNITY FINDING**

3. Make sense of these items. How can they really change your vision?

4. Integrating these few high-impact and high-probability drivers of your future, create three stories: a best-case story where most things go your way, a worst-case story were most things don't go your way, and the middle story where some things go your way and some things don't.

5. Finally, for each story, identify a few things that will tell you if you are on course or off course as you go along—find the red flags. For example, if you need a loan to start a new small business but leading financial experts have identified that the economy may be heading for recession, you might want to postpone your plans until capital is available or seek an alternative way of funding your vision.

As time goes on, revisit the scenarios and adjust them. Pay close attention to where you are getting the future right and where you are missing things. If you find you are overly optimistic, enlist a friend who's a bit of a pessimist, or vice versa. The future is fluid and ever-changing, so be prepared to adapt to it in real time as appropriate.

The Artist Is Not a
Lone Genius

It's time to reimagine the Artist not as a lone genius who works deep into the night on a riotously ambitious project, but as an ordinary man or woman with the tools and colleagues to make something happen. This is the insight Tom learned along the way while adapting to the world around him: you can be an Artist anywhere as long as you adjust your vision to the needs of others. In modifying your own vision, you'll be able to see everyone else's even better. Don't be the Tom who goes to Broadway—be the Tom who creates his own Broadway.

The Artist

DESCRIPTION

As an Artist, you are clever and creative. You envision change, so your influence is based on anticipating a better future and generating hope in others. You actively pursue innovation and adaptation. You are driven to express yourself in spontaneous, creative responses to your surroundings. You are imaginative, able to handle a high degree of ambiguity, and comfortable with abstract ideas. You believe success is being original, expressing new ideas, and prototyping those ideas when possible.

CHARACTERISTICS

You tend to...
- Take risks
- Incite change
- Focus on the future
- Discover opportunities
- Envision new products or services
- Experiment through pilot projects
- Test boundaries
- Find new ways of doing things

EXAMPLES

- Larry Page (CEO of Google)
- Jeff Bezos (CEO of Amazon)
- Peter Diamandis (CEO of XPRIZE Foundation)
- Elon Musk (CEO of Tesla)

STRENGTHS

- Creative, artistic, expressive, imaginative
- Flexible, adaptive
- Optimistic, enthusiastic
- Accept failure, take risks
- Future-oriented
- Conceptual

WEAKNESSES

- Ignore and break rules
- Rebellious, impulsive, undisciplined
- Unfocused, distracted
- Unable to make realistic plans
- Take too many risks
- Rush to actions

SKILLS TO DEVELOP

1. **Pay Attention to Details**
   Yes, details are cumbersome and not a lot of fun. But sometimes you have to do mundane things in order to give yourself the freedom to innovate. Take some time to think things through, so you can learn from your experience and craft a better experiment next time. It helps you become smarter and innovate more effectively.
2. **Work With the System—Not Against It**
   You always find a way around rules and procedures, but not all rules are bad. You need to learn to see the underlying reasons for those rules. While you don't always have to follow them, you need to respect and consider them before you take unnecessary risks or put others in danger.
3. **Develop Your Communication Skills**
   You need the help of other people to fulfill your vision. As great as it may be, your vision won't come true if you cannot help other people see it. Take some time to revise the vision you see. You will grow much more if you take account of other people's viewpoints and incorporate them into your own vision.

FIGURE 2. **THE ARTIST (continued on next page)**

FIGURE 2. **THE ARTIST (continued from previous page)**

HOW TO TALK TO AN ARTIST

- Look at the big picture
- Draw concepts
- Use metaphors
- Look toward the future
- Take risks and conduct experiments

	IF YOU ARE AN ARTIST	IF YOUR ORGANIZATION IS AN ARTIST
THEN...	You will create value through your ability to turn creative risk into growth projects.	Value is created through the creation of systems, spaces, and structures that support the generation and execution of ideas, creativity, and divergence.
AND YOU WORK WITH SAGES	Your relationship with them will succeed when there is an emphasis on trying new things, coming up with new ideas, and learning from them in a supportive manner.	Your organization will successfully create value with others through long-term joint ventures or large-scale innovation projects to generate new knowledge.
AND YOU WORK WITH ATHLETES	Your relationship with them will succeed when there is a mutual emphasis on generating attention (or cheerleading) for a common visible project.	Your organization will successfully create value with others when a partnership generates capital for large, visible, and highly innovative, growth projects.
AND YOU WORK WITH ENGINEERS	The difficulties in your relationship with them will center on matters of risk. Your big ideas will likely be perceived as too risky. All projects have some degree of risk, so you must direct your efforts toward outlining reasonable risks and reasonably foreseeable rewards in an analytical way.	Your organization will have a difficult time because of conflicting perspectives on balancing and evaluating functional risk and reward. Look for common ground that represents reasonable risk but yields significant growth potential. You may consider forming smaller scale alliances for specific targets instead of a larger partnership.

Summary

Artists are radical visionaries who constantly want to try new things. They tend to work on several projects at the same time and can easily get distracted, but they ultimately incite meaningful change and take risks others would shy away from. They can grow by adding more structure to their projects, making priorities, and finding ways to work within the system.

Exercise

In the spirit of constructive conflict, let's temper the pure creative energy of an Artist by thinking like the opposite—like an Engineer. To make your ideas and plans more viable, try converging and operationalizing the possibilities by asking the following *CONTROL* questions:

- **C**redibility: How would we get credibility with stakeholders to pursue this idea?
- **O**bjective: What can we do to ensure that our decisions are based on facts?
- **N**ecessary: What can we do to pinpoint what is most important?
- **T**ime: What are the timelines for pursuing this idea?
- **R**esources: What money and other resources are required to pursue this idea?
- **O**rder: What can we do to manage our project in the most efficient sequence?
- **L**ogic: What can we do to methodically think through our options?

CHAPTER 6

The Engineer

Aabha always had two plans. She had the plan for what she wanted to do—and the plan for what she thought she should do. She loved visual arts, but she also loved logical reasoning. A dreamer with a fondness for pragmatism, she was pulled in two different directions.

Her parents had always encouraged her to follow her passions, no matter how fanciful they seemed to her, so she studied Art History at a top Canadian university. After graduation, she found herself immediately underemployed. Her instinct for safer planning kicked in. Reluctantly, with only one year in the real world behind her, she continued on to law school, where she graduated with distinction.

At school, Aabha met her future husband Rajeev, who was finishing his medical degree. Despite her lack of enthusiasm for the profession she was spending three years preparing to enter, Aabha found that her talents made her an excellent lawyer.

Underwhelmed by the prospect of a life in law, Aabha halfheart-edly accepted a job at a top white-shoe firm in New York while Rajeev did his residency in cardiology at a nearby medical center. They were the poster couple on the rise.

Aabha found life at the law firm paralyzing. She worked con-stantly for bosses who mistreated her. The ruthless partners never gave her sufficient time to properly prep her cases and frequently berated her, expecting her to sacrifice her personal life for the benefit of the practice just like they had. With Rajeev perpetually on call at the hospital, the couple had very little time together. On the rare occasions her colleagues had the time to get together after work for a beer, they'd complain about their mean-spirited taskmasters but seemed to find the sweatshop experience strange-ly exhilarating.

Aabha finally found a like-minded ally when she was assigned to a project with a seasoned attorney named Chetana. Also Indian, Chetana admitted that working under the blue-blood boys could be oppressive but noted that things had improved considerably over the years. They met to discuss the case every other day over afternoon tea. When Aabha confessed that she was seriously con-sidering leaving the firm, Chetana observed how similar the two were and encouraged her to find ways of incorporating her per-sonal interests into her work and stay on until she reached partner.

Reenergized by the friendship, Aabha worked diligently to win the case, which dragged on over a year before it was success-fully settled. One afternoon, Aabha stopped by Chetana's office to share an idea to add an art litigation practice to the firm that would enhance their ability to gain both institutional and estate deals. Aabha saw it as an opportunity for the firm to grow a new line of business and a way for her to bring her personal passion for art to the office. Chetana smiled and said, "I'm sorry, but I can't take this to the partners. We both know that they will never go for it. It just isn't a priority for the firm." Silent and broken, Aabha left the office. Three days later, she quit. Chetana called and left a warm invitation to talk, but Aabha never returned the call.

After weeks of second-guessing herself, Aabha went to work with a friend who owned a trendy art gallery in Soho. She enjoyed her work but found that things moved a bit slower than she preferred. Months passed, and she had all but forgotten her legal career when she received a phone call from Chetana asking if she'd be interested in taking a case as an adjunct member of her team. The firm was representing a Latin American museum that was suing a deposed dictator to recover some jewelry and other treasures of historical significance. After considerable reflection and subsequent hesitation, Aabha took the case. Surprisingly, she found the work engaging and was shocked by how much she now liked collaborating with her old colleagues from the law firm.

The project inspired her to start a boutique legal practice that specialized in matters of art. Aabha loved the independence that came from her sole proprietorship and the interdependence that the affiliation with the company brought. She had found her own voice, her real expertise, her bliss. The two plans she'd had from the beginning and the two passions she'd long convinced herself were simply incompatible had come together in an unexpectedly satisfying way.

The Luminous Pragmatism of Engineers

She may not want to admit it, but Aabha is an Engineer through and through. All of the qualities that make her a stellar lawyer—her luminous pragmatism, her methodical approach to problem solving, her penchant for objectivity, and her astonishing persistence—are the characteristics that define anyone with this dominant worldview. That she is a reluctant Engineer makes her all the more perfect as a model. For Engineers are much more complicated than the number-crunching, by-the-book people we might expect them to be. They are thoughtful, sensitive thinkers—as creative as Artists—yet they thrive in environments with procedures and established ways of doing things.

Engineers are systematic, disciplined team members. They embrace reliability as they work to eliminate deviance. They love to take preexisting ideas and products and make them into something bigger—something reproducible, global, universal. What they seek is efficiency. They strive for incremental innovations. They want quality—foolproof systems that can make a lot out of something already proven to be great.

At the organizational level, the Engineer organization is a large-scale company with many rules and structured, hierarchical ways of doing things. Since the organization's growth is driven by process, it is easily scalable. Think Dell Computer. Think McDonald's. Think Boeing and Toyota. Think British Petroleum. For these companies, failure is not an option. They are companies that make their money on scale. In these companies, you will always find complexity—there are many parts to manage. This is a slow-moving, low-risk kind of growth. It certainly won't change the game, but it is most definitely a growth you can count on.

Taken too far, Engineers become control freaks. It's the sweatshop sensibility that Aabha hated most about her law firm: the unthinking celebration of productivity at all costs. That Aabha could see the dark side of this in her colleagues makes her an especially self-aware Engineer. Indeed, her impulse to bring some creativity into the firm was a great one—for the people that Engineers need most in their lives are the ones most of them have the least in common with: Artists.

Artists and Engineers have a lot to teach each other. While Artists shake up the rules of Engineers, Engineers minimize the chaos of Artists.

What Engineers show everyone is that an innovation doesn't have to be radical in order to be meaningful or worthwhile. It's often better to think smaller and look at what's already out there. Instead of trying to find something no one has seen before, Engineers create extensions of current solutions. They take something that already exists and make it a little different or better. They apply more effective uses of low-cost, low-level systems and technologies to transform an old service into a more efficient one. The key idea is not newer but better, cheaper, and faster.

The Understated Genius of an Engineer's Innovation

We often discount or dismiss the kind of innovation that Engineers call for because it doesn't sound exciting enough. Cool, shiny, and sleek: these are the qualities we associate with top-shelf innovations. That's because we're constantly confronted with magazines and Internet lists of the most innovative companies that are essentially just beauty contests. At the top of all these shimmering lists are blustery bands, glitzy gadgets, and chic designers.

But take a closer look and you'll see that these sparkly objects aren't really the best innovations. The most valuable innovations don't have extraordinary stories and they're not cool, shiny, or sleek. They're plain and understated, they blend in with their surroundings—they're the inventions that don't catch our eye. They're hidden in plain sight.

That's the great insight that Engineers have to offer the world: true innovation happens behind the scenes. Sure, new technologies, products, and services that we perceive as breakthrough advancements look exciting, but the meaningful innovation is in the larger, more complicated processes that make those things possible.

There's no new miracle drug without discoveries in chemistry, manufacturing, and control processes. There's no new animated feature film without a revolution in software-coding practices. There's no new electric car without developments in material sciences.

The Engineers are the people who make this kind of growth and development happen. They're the underrated back-office superstars—quiet, diligent individuals working out of public view, often in bureaucratic departments. These are the people who can see where the dots connect, who can tell where there are opportunities for change.

Think of the structure of any large organization in terms of a mid-office and a back-office staff. Mid-office members have leadership positions like Chief of Staff and Operating Officer. The back-office members work in Legal, Financial, Information Technology, and Human Resources departments. All of the units in any office are vertically oriented so that everyone reports to their own sector's manager. The few places in an organization that are also horizontally oriented are these back-office departments. Here, people can look *across* the business: thanks to their back-office viewpoint, Engineers see where the points of contact are between all the parts of the larger company.

Example:
The Back-Office Triumph of a Wall Street Bank

It is this back-office kind of thinking that helped spark a wildly successful innovation in a large, well-respected Wall Street investment bank at a key moment of transition.

When the director of executive training first noticed his company was in a crisis, it was the end of the go-go '90s, when all of the mega-mergers were ending, and all of the powerful investment firms were looking for new ways to make money. This venerable old banking institution was out of position: while other banks were experimenting with different strategies or trying to put together mergers, this bank had stayed traditional, maintaining the same structure it had relied on for nearly one hundred years.

As a result of this dependence on the old way of doing things, the company was disjointed. Each of its locations around the world was successful, but there was very little—if any—communication between each of those locations. Now, the executives wanted its regional chief financial officers to be more active in advising the leaders at the center of the company, to be more anticipatory and responsive in planning for the future.

Soon, with the help of some Engineers' perspectives and the push and pull of constructive conflict, the director recognized that there was an opportunity for a new source of revenue—a previously untapped area of income: the strategies developed by the legal team and other behind-the-scenes sectors. These back-office teams of Engineers had come up with effective solutions to the company's problems, to issues that many other big global companies face. In particular, they had mastered the process of moving their branches from one location to another, relocating from one area to a new one without creating a lot of exposure. They had discovered the legal tax maneuverings and the offshoring techniques necessary to mitigating risk.

The company went on to take these winning ideas and strategies developed by back-office members and repackaged them so they could sell them as a service to other industries.

The issue was that the main controllers and financial officers of the organization were simply not aware of how their company worked, what went on behind the scenes. Once they learned what they could do with these invaluable sources of creativity, they made use of these back-office strategies. The back office started creating a book of business policies and sold it worldwide.

This new initiative brought in a huge amount of revenue for the banking firm. While some businesses that bought these strategies didn't replicate the original success, many—especially those in similar cultural environments—did recreate that success.

The point is this: everyone always talks to the new technology people and the trend experts—the Artists—when they want to achieve radical innovation, but the people you should talk to first are the ones in your own back office—the Engineers. These are the people who really know where and how the business comes together. They see the opportunities for growth before anyone else does. They are the ones who can search for and reapply great ideas quickly. Don't look far for new talent. Your brightest stars are likely already in your backyard.

Exercise:
Rapid Prototyping

You don't have to be technically proficient or intensely disciplined to think or see the world like an Engineer. In the Engineer's spirit of rulemaking and rule following, there are easy ways to reproduce the skillset of these methodical innovators. If you can't find or recruit an Engineer—or just need that reliable kind of incremental growth for yourself—here is an exercise for tapping into your own inner Engineer.

When launching any new project, it's best to start with a prototype because you want to prove the concept works before you spend a lot of time and resources. What you want to do is to develop the idea as quickly as possible so as to minimize expenses and risk. Then, learn what really works and what really doesn't, both in the making and selling of the idea. And finally, make adjustments to advance to full-scale production.

Prototyping any idea, both products and services, as well as any solution that enhances our own lives, is a highly iterative process: version one, version two, and so on. It is unlikely that you will get it right on the first try. One of the biggest mistakes people make when launching a new project is to get stuck in the planning cycle where we spend too much time strategizing and not enough time testing our ideas in the real world. Use the followings steps to develop your prototype:

1. Create criteria for success. What is required is that we engage in the constructive conflict of the four dominant worldviews to develop a shared and clear definition of the results we seek from our prototype including specific target number, benchmark, and resources:

    -   Artist: a unique, never-before-seen, one-of-a-kind prototype
    -   Engineer: a predictable, works-everywhere, turnkey solution prototype
    -   Athlete: a valuable, defeats-your-competitors, first-to-market prototype
    -   Sage: a principled, mission-affirming, community-sustainable prototype

2. Prioritize the features you need. Make a list of the most essential features from the point of view of your target market. For example, if our idea is to commercialize our grandmother's recipe for Italian spaghetti sauce, it makes sense to focus your efforts on testing the sauce in restaurants first before you move on to concerns of marketing, manufacturing, and distribution. If you don't get the first step right, there will be no second step. Ask yourself the following questions for each feature you are considering:

    -   How important is this feature to the success of the prototype?

- How many potential customers will find this feature essential?
- Will this feature determine the success or failure of this prototype?
- Are there substitutes for this feature that are cheaper, faster, or better?
- How much value does this feature bring to the prototype?

3. Develop a Minimal Viable Product (MVP). Working with the list of features, get your prototype into production quickly and inexpensively. Trade-offs are inevitable at this stage, and you must consider the best available option to get your prototype into production. New information and technology have made prototyping easier, faster, and less expensive than ever. Prototypes can be made in a number of ways from the very inexpensive to the very expensive, from simple pencil sketches to 3-D printing. The objective is to spend as little time and money as possible because the real aim of this phase is to accelerate learning so that adjustments can be made in future versions.

4. Find what worked and what didn't. Use the constructive conflict from the four worldviews to make innovative adjustments to the prototype. In addition, establish some simple rules of thumb, based on the real information gleaned from the prototype, to be implemented going forward. This way, you learn from your mistakes instead of repeating them in the next version.

5. Develop your next version. It may take several attempts and versions before you have a scalable prototype.

6. Finally, once you have a viable prototype, you need to find the most efficient and effective way to operationalize it to scale. How this is done is primarily dependent upon the

goal of the prototype. For example, if the aim of the prototype was to create a blog on the Internet, getting the site up and some initial network marketing in place may be all that is needed. On the other hand, if your grandmother's spaghetti sauce turns out to be a winner in the prototype phase, you may need to start marketing efforts with food companies and restaurants, or alternatively negotiations with banks, financiers, manufacturers, and distributors.

Prototyping is a great way to minimize risk while learning what works and what doesn't. The key is to spend as few resources as possible in the shortest time possible. It's a way to accelerate failure, not to avoid it. If your first prototype doesn't work, that's fine. The information you get from making it and running that experiment will help you in the future. The sooner you get results, the better off you are. Remember to develop and evaluate your prototypes from the four dominant worldviews. And like climbing stairs, take it one step at a time.

The Artistry in
Engineers

While the Engineer is almost the precise opposite of the Artist, there is an art to the precision and commitment to procedure that the Engineer brings to any project, an art just as brilliant and powerful as the Artist's wild fantasy of the future. Behind all of the rules, efficiency, and methodical reliability is an imaginative vision. The rules and the vision can and do coexist if the Engineer plays it right. The triumph is seeing the compatibility of the two things Aabha always thought were completely at odds with each other: the plan of our dreams and the plan of our needs.

The Engineer

DESCRIPTION

As an Engineer, you are a well-informed technical expert. You are diligent, meticulous, and function-based. You monitor, track, and document details. You influence others based on the control and management of information. Improving efficiency through process redesign and the implementation of reliable technology is your hallmark. You define success as improving quality through the use of procedures. You are risk averse and seek to take variation out of the system, valuing standardization and consistency. You use a lot of rational measurements and love data.

CHARACTERISTICS

You tend to...
- Apply technical expertise
- Analyze and manage data
- Make incremental improvements
- Refine methods and processes
- Develop policies and procedures
- Establish technological systems
- Maintain the structure and flow of work
- Influence through objective information

EXAMPLES

- Michael Bloomberg (former mayor of New York City)
- Alan Mulally (former CEO of Ford)
- Xi Jinping (President of the People's Republic of China)
- Warren Buffett (CEO of Berkshire Hathaway)

STRENGTHS

- Logical, rational, objective
- Organized, orderly, methodical
- Follow rules and procedures
- Safe, reliable, dependable
- Productive, efficient
- Disciplined, persistent

WEAKNESSES

- Authoritarian, controlling
- Inflexible, rigid, dogmatic, stubborn
- Uncreative, no new ideas
- Resistant to change
- Hierarchical, bureaucratic
- Focused on details only, not the big picture

SKILLS TO DEVELOP

I. Avoid Overthinking Decisions
Sometimes you need to make a decision without enough data or act without fully knowing all the risks. Opportunities may vanish if you take too long and hesitate. It's okay if you make a mistake or your action ends in failure. You need to learn from those failures to make you smarter for next time. Ease yourself into this by trying something new where failure won't matter very much.

2. Develop Flexibility
To succeed in times of rapid change, you need to develop your tolerance for ambiguity and flexibility. Accept that you may need to correct your course as you get more information about a new issue. You need to incorporate new information as it emerges and be flexible on your journey.

3. Pay More Attention to People and Not Just Processes
Even though outcomes and processes are important, people are the ones who get the work done. Learn to empower your team and lessen your dependence on hierarchy. Solicit their participation, ideas, and perspectives.

HOW TO TALK TO AN ENGINEER

- Provide details
- Follow the rules
- Explain things in sequential order
- Conform to the common spirit of the group
- Demonstrate how things work to others

	IF YOU ARE AN ENGINEER	**IF YOUR ORGANIZATION IS AN ENGINEER**
THEN...	You will create value through your attention to detail and your ability to recognize incremental opportunities.	Value is created when it connects practices, processes, and systems with growth objectives.
AND YOU WORK WITH SAGES	Your relationship with them will succeed when you place a collective emphasis on learning to do things the right way.	Your organization will successfully create value with others when you create long-term and trusting relationships that build industry knowledge and practices.

FIGURE 3. **THE ENGINEER (continued on next page)**

FIGURE 3. **THE ENGINEER (continued from previous page)**

AND YOU WORK WITH ATHLETES	Your relationship with them will succeed when there is a mutual interest in minimizing some sort of risk.	Your organization will successfully create value with others when there are clear goals, timelines, responsibilities, and outcomes.
AND YOU WORK WITH ARTISTS	The difficulties in your relationship with them will center on matters of risk. Others will perceive your assessment of risk and caution as an obstruction of ideas and progress. Make sure your concerns are reasonable and look for ways to turn these concerns into opportunities for new ideas.	Your organization will have a difficult time because of conflicting views on balancing and evaluating risk and reward. You must recognize that some risk is necessary for growth. Look for common ground that represents reasonable risk but yields significant growth potential. You may consider very specific arrangements instead of a long-term relationship.

Summary

Reliable and logical, Engineers like to make things work very efficiently. They rely on processes and procedures to produce the highest quality products and services every time, everywhere. They can grow by reducing their tendency to pore over data and pushing themselves to seize an opportunity when it presents itself. The challenge is for Engineers to embrace their inner Artist and learn to be more comfortable with ambiguity and the unknown.

Exercise

Harness the energy of constructive conflict by taking all your Engineer-like impulses and filtering them through the lens of an Artist. To make your ideas and plans more creative, try diverging and expanding the possibilities by asking the following *CREATE* questions:

- **C**ombine: What if we combined this with something else?
- **R**everse: What if we did the opposite?
- **E**xpand: What if we made it larger?
- **A**dapt: What if we changed some part of this?
- **T**rim: What if we made it smaller?
- **E**xchange: What if we traded places with something else?

CHAPTER 7

When Artists and Engineers Meet: An Exercise in Constructive Conflict

Artists are highly imaginative and pulled forward by their big-picture vision. Engineers are objectively scientific and driven by processes that provide data and direction. While Artists are stronger in conceptualizing radical new ideas, Engineers are better at making them work and putting them into operation. So the way to harness the strengths of both is to start with an Artistic vision and end with an Engineer's detailed plan.

Metaphors are comparisons between two things that are usually unrelated. In essence, they allow us to make complex connections simple and legible. For example, when we see a television commercial comparing drinking a soda to jumping into a swimming pool on a hot summer day, we make the unmistakable connection that the drink is refreshing. Using metaphors to connect large, unrelated ideas is typically a strength of the Artist.

Conversely, metaphors can be used to make the simple complex. Using the same example, there are many functions and attributes associated with a swimming pool that do not immediately come to mind when thinking about drinking a soda: a diving board, swimming attire, or chlorine. By connecting those aspects that are not readily associated, the metaphor becomes more detailed and operational, a strong suit of the Engineer. As such, metaphors are an effective way to constructively unite these two oppositional dominant worldviews.

In this exercise, we'll use metaphors to create a hybrid solution combining both the Artist and Engineer dominant worldviews:

1. State your challenge. This can either be an opportunity you wish to capture or a problem you wish to solve.

2. Pick a few metaphors and experiment with them. Below are a few to get you started:
   - Planting a garden
   - Spreading a rumor
   - Getting a date
   - Calculating a tip
   - Buckling seatbelts
   - Paying taxes
   - Preparing for a marathon

3. Ask yourself: How is our challenge like this metaphor? Use the free-association technique to look for any and all

connections, both obvious and not-so-obvious ones. Suspend your voice of judgment. Be sure to write your ideas down so you don't lose them.

4. Once you find a metaphor that works and fully develop it, turn it inside-out. For example, let's say your challenge is how to get into a top-rated college, and you've selected planting a garden as your metaphor. You've made the obvious connections between the metaphor and the challenge, such as the need to plant a diverse mixture of vegetables at the proper time and applying to a wide array of institutions, some for early admission while others for standard admission. After you have considered the conspicuous connections, look for functions and attributes of planting a garden that are inconspicuous: soil pH, sources of water, frost damage, or financial constraints. This force-fitting of the details associated with planting a garden makes the potential solution to the challenge more comprehensive and easier to put into operation.

5. Finally, translate the various elements of the solution into an action plan. For example, the metaphor of making sure the soil pH is optimal for growing your crops might translate into applying to those schools whose admission standards are best suited for your credentials. The first step in your action plan may be to gather information on the admission criteria of top schools and to focus only on those often overlooked and where your application is likely to flourish.

By using metaphors, you can capitalize on the constructive conflict between the large-scale vision of the artist and the operational detail of the engineer to produce innovative solutions that are both original and practical.

CHAPTER 8

The Athlete

It wasn't the kids that brought Gary to Kung Fu. When his friends found out he was opening a training studio for students, they were beyond surprised. Gary wasn't exactly a people person, let alone good with kids. During his time in the military, when he first discovered his passion for Kung Fu, he was a bit of a lone ranger. So, to those who knew him, the thought of Gary surrounded by eager, impressionable kids was unimaginable, comical—even preposterous.

Gary and his students were studies in almost cartoonish contrasts. The kids were in it for the fun while Gary was in it for the ancient Chinese precepts that had drawn him to the martial art as a soldier: the strict adherence to a code of personal conduct and the self-denial. The youngsters who enrolled in Gary's class were far from the serious, disciplined pupils he expected. They were simply kids brought by their parents, looking for a good time.

Despite his students' understandably fun-loving spirits, Gary taught the kids the only way he knew how—the same way he had learned martial arts: through systematic repetition, subordination, and self-discipline. The children struggled, cried, and left the program. At first, Gary was disappointed that these kids showed no perseverance and that their parents had enabled this behavior. But when his own children had the same reaction to his training, Gary began to rethink his entire approach.

Gary started with a simple question: How would Kung Fu be improved if it were developed today? He realized he needed to go against all of his usual impulses. He resisted his typical self-sufficiency, impatience, and stubbornness and sought out the help of others to answer this question.

Cold Gary warmed up. He talked with parents who told him that, even though they'd signed their kids up for Kung Fu as a low-stakes hobby, they still wanted their children to develop self-will, respect for others, and the confidence that they could defend themselves if necessary.

Gary also did some research and discovered that soccer, swimming, and dancing were the most popular organized activities with kids. He had a theory that these pastimes created a real sense of belonging and community that children used to get from their church or neighborhood.

If Gary's friends were shocked when they heard about his plan to teach kids, they were downright stunned when Gary enrolled in some child psychology courses at the local community college. The taskmaster was now a student himself. He supplemented his new education with a wide array of personal achievement audio programs. He developed a deeply insightful point of view about how positive reinforcement was far more effective than some of the traditional methods of martial arts training.

Gradually, Gary began to create an entirely new way to teach the essential ideas and techniques of Kung Fu to kids. He started by enlisting the help of family and friends who had skills wildly different than his own: elementary school teachers, stay-at-home moms, and entertainers, to name a few. He then developed an entire curriculum dependent on the constant positive reinforcement of parents and peers. The tough-as-nails military vet suddenly saw the necessity of frequent awards ceremonies, smaller teams for specific interests, and a lot of "you can do it" attitude and applause.

Soon, the former lone ranger became an unlikely coauthor. One student's parent was a writer and asked to ghostwrite a workbook about Gary's method. A local best seller, the book was the beginning of something much bigger: an entire school of thought adopted by others. Now, children and parents were enrolling in the programs in large numbers, and other martial arts instructors were seeking advice from Gary. All the while Gary was growing into a new type of master—compassionate, patient, and perceptive. The only person more surprised than his friends was Gary himself.

The Athlete and the Desire to Win at All Costs

The aggressive competitor in his perpetual one-man game, Gary is an archetypal Athlete. Peel back the layer of his newfound compassion and patience and you find the qualities that define anyone with this dominant worldview: a cutthroat instinct, the thirst for quick returns, a Darwinist worldview, and the desire to win— often at all costs. All of the things Gary learned *not* to do as a Kung Fu teacher are the things that make him a successful Athlete.

Athletes are forceful leaders who are driven by profit and speed. They are masters at image-enhancement and deal-making. They thrive in high-pressure environments with quantifiable results. What they seek is power. They reach it by looking at everything that comes their way as a challenge, an opportunity to do something bigger and better than anyone who's done it before.

At the organizational level, Athletic companies create an atmosphere of winners and losers, where the competitive spirit of laissez-faire capitalism rules. These organizations want strong results, and they want them fast. That's why they value people based on their output. Think Microsoft. Think Goldman Sachs. Think General Electric. These are companies that will produce revenue under any and all circumstances. It's not enough for them to be successful—they have to be on top.

In their determined bid for domination bordering on annihilation, Athletes are shortsighted. They win the immediate round but fail to see the long game. Too eager for the instant victory, they don't have the patience to build the kind of community and culture that sustain durable growth.

For this reason, every Athlete needs a Sage—a teacher or facilitator who can slow them down and temper their sometimes abrasive concern for the current moment. The Sage brings empathy and interpersonal acuity into the otherwise ruthless boardroom. The killer instinct of an Athlete and the social intelligence of a Sage is a dynamite combination. This is the life-changing insight that made Gary come out on top: he needed the feedback of others to learn what his students actually wanted. With this awareness, Gary won the game that actually mattered—the one that lasted long enough for a whole new generation of martial artists to learn his methods.

Courage
under Fire

We can all use a little Athleticism on our teams when the moment calls for it. The great gift of Athletes is their courage—their willingness to do anything for a win. The remarkability of Athletes' bravery lies not just in what they're prepared to do but also in what they're prepared to sacrifice. It's the difficulty that innovators often overlook: it's harder to stop doing something old than it is to start doing something new. The ease with which Athletes give up things that aren't working is something we should all adopt in our innovation initiatives.

Example:
A News Agency on
the Verge of Collapse

Occasional reminiscence is good for the mind and soul, but too much looking backward prevents progress. Excess nostalgia can turn into hoarding—when the past pushes out the future. This is almost always unintentional. There are tons of organizations that inadvertently stifle innovation by fixating on the past, placing too much emphasis on classics and standards.

This was exactly the situation faced by an international news agency close to bankruptcy, in an industry that was changing more quickly than they could keep up with. All the time they spent focusing on their own senior management and maintaining their traditions, they failed to pay attention to the trends emerging in the world around them. The company needed a new start.

It began with the company's annual meeting. Usually an event held in a sunny tropical place where the organization's best and brightest could enjoy themselves as they celebrated their successes, the annual meeting this year would be something very different, held at a warehouse in the agency's home city, in a large open space with no chairs, where everyone would stand as they cultivated an innovative mindset.

The organization created a frenetic, experimental space where individuals from all levels and sectors talked through the five central problems that they collectively diagnosed: the speed at which the organization moved, the adoption of new technology, the development of a twenty-first-century workforce, big data, and client management.

As discussions continued, it became clear that everybody had a very strong desire to win and a determination to make things work. They made plans that they believed would turn things around and put them on top. On the second day, the firm successfully determined precisely what kind of talent it would need to make all of these plans a reality. Everyone took ownership of their responsibilities and made a commitment to each other, spelling out the concrete steps they would take as individuals to contribute to these larger efforts. The energy and desire to win were palpable in the room.

At the end of the summit, one of the organization's most talented thinkers stood up. He had entered the retreat with huge skepticism and had prepared his official resignation prior to it. In front of everyone, he ripped his resignation into many pieces and threw them all around him. The session had been so promising and encouraging to him that he not only abandoned all plans to resign but also publicly pledged to buy thousands of shares of the company. He sat down and someone else stood up, doubling his pledge. Next, one of the organization's top leaders vowed to buy triple the shares. The spark of hope spread through the room like a wildfire. It was the Athletic spirit that launched the energy needed to look forward to new fights and new wins.

The end of the story is a happy one, but the year after the retreat was simply awful. Rebuilding the company from the inside out required major downsizing. This meant tons of layoffs and restructuring. In short, the organization had to give up a lot in order to reinvent itself. The next twelve months were painful, yet the outcome was overwhelmingly positive. In the next year, the company saw itself at the top of the industry.

The greatest growth and change don't happen when executives are comfortably sipping wine in a scenic abbey—it happens when everyone is forced to start over together in an empty warehouse. Innovation hurts. There is no way around this fact: innovation entails tough sacrifices in often drastic circumstances. It's harder to stop doing old things than it is to start doing new things. The first step of all innovations is destruction. For this reason, innovation takes something much bigger than creativity: courage. What Athletes show us is that, when it comes to innovation, ingenuity and resourcefulness are overrated. Capacity and courage are what will always win the game.

Exercise:
Portfolio Managing

In their ever-impatient search for the next win, Athletes are constantly evaluating what's in front of them, what's working, and what's not working. They look at everything like a portfolio: weighing the advantages and disadvantages of all of the elements in their projects and seeing which makes the most sense to pursue. They know how to weed out projects that aren't worth their time.

It's this portfolio way of thinking that is an Athlete's best asset. Forget what you've heard about comparing apples to oranges. It's often helpful to put your organization's diverse projects alongside each other and compare them as if they were competing in a race. We can even use this technique to evaluate different things we are doing in our lives. This is the point of maintaining a portfolio: to treat initiatives like investments and to weigh them against each other, balancing and maximizing the relative worth of these projects through disciplined decision-making and resource allocation.

The challenge is that everything in this world costs something. The fact is, most of us want what we don't possess now but fail to consider what we must give up to get it. It's not that we can't have it all. In fact, we can. It's the cost of having it all that we are unwilling to acknowledge. Our capacity is bound by time and resources. We are all in the perpetual state of being overbooked. This is because it's easy to start new things. It's hard to stop old things because they represent our commitments and sense of duty to those we love. It's not just about us as individuals. We live in families and communities where our changes ultimately become theirs.

The key is to reallocate our resources, time, and energy according to what we really seek now. While stopping the old is the hardest of all the decisions, it is the most important because it makes room for the new. Remember that the world around us greatly enables or inhibits our decisions, so pay attention to which way the proverbial wind is blowing.

When prioritizing, remember that the importance of any task is relative to the other tasks that need to be performed. Think of it like a checkbook. The most important bills get paid first. Use the following steps to rebalance your portfolio:

1. Look at your schedule over a two- or three-week period of time and make a list of all the tasks you currently perform. Now add to that list all the new tasks and projects you intend to start in the near future.

2. Create a table like the one below (Table 5). Use the Y-axis to represent the amount of effort to complete the task and the X-axis for the amount of payoff you expect.

	EASY TO IMPLEMENT	TOUGH TO IMPLEMENT
SMALL PAY-OFF	**SMALL WINS**	**TIME-WASTERS**
BIG PAY-OFF	**BIG WINS**	**SPECIAL CASES**

TABLE 5. **SELECTING PROJECTS**

3. Analyze each task in the list and place it in the appropriate cell in the table:

- Big Wins: tasks and commitments that bring great success and are easy to do
- Small Wins: tasks and commitments that bring incremental success and are easy to do
- Special Cases: tasks and commitments that bring great success and are difficult to do
- Time Wasters: tasks and commitments that bring incremental success and are hard to do

Big Wins should always be pursued first because they create the most success for the least amount of effort. Small Wins should be pursued next because they create incremental success and build momentum. Special Cases should be pursued with caution because they typically take far more resources and time than anticipated. There should be no more than one or two of these in the portfolio. Time Wasters should be abandoned, handed off, or dissolved if possible.

Portfolio management requires looking at all possibilities, including the ones that typically fall outside of our own dominant worldview. This requires that we give serious consideration to those initiatives we typically deem less valuable. Constructive conflict is inherent in the prioritization process because the value of each project is relative to the others. This structured decision-making process also allows for us to adjust or re-create our projects into new or hybrid forms. Use the portfolio approach not only to focus on key goals and accelerate their attainment but also to create a balanced portfolio life.

For all the fast, reliable results of portfolio management, there are some downsides. A portfolio sometimes creates too few projects, depends on biased criteria, and encourages myopic thinking. Keep these pitfalls in mind as you make portfolio management work for you.

The Games around Us

This Darwinist model is what fuels and inspires Athletes. They approach everything they do as if it were a game. It is a worldview we can all benefit from. Conceptualizing innovation projects as high-stakes competitions for the future will not only give your team motivation—it will also give a strategic edge. For the reality is that innovation *is* a game, and your industry peers *are* your rivals. So part of the game is realizing that you're in a game. The organizations that don't even realize they're in a competition are always the first losers.

The long-term key to winning is having a strategic edge over your competitors—a playbook that can anticipate the future before everyone else. You can't actually know the future, but you can feel your way toward it by running many experiments at once and consulting data that can predict what happens in the future. Athletes are expert strategists, which is why they win so often.

But in their unquenchable thirst for instant victory, Athletes miss the larger game. They fail to understand that the game is an end in itself. Sure, all innovations have many finite games built into them, yet there is no real end to the competition.

In James P. Carse's classic *Finite and Infinite Games,* he posits that finite games have a definite beginning and ending, clear boundaries and rules, and winners and losers of the contest. In essence, these games are engaging because all of the elements of competition are known, and nothing new needs to be discovered. These are the kinds of games that Athletes crave, the ones where they can rely on their old playbook to win. Recall Gary's original approach to Kung Fu instruction: repeating the same winning methods that worked for him.

Conversely, infinite games do not have a knowable beginning or ending; they are played with the intent to keep playing, discovering, and learning new things—to keep adding new players to the game. The most winning Athlete is not the one who comes in first every time but the one who reimagines the game itself and becomes more sensitive to the other players. Gary was at the top as a Kung Fu master, yet he didn't master the teaching of it until he reconceived his approach. And, though his school became a runaway success, he acknowledged that he must remain open-minded to new alternatives and emerging trends. A good Athlete can knock out his opponent. A great Athlete can beat his own record. An exceptional Athlete can adapt to a new game even when the rules aren't clear. Play on at your own risk. The game's afoot.

The Athlete ⚬

DESCRIPTION

As an Athlete, you are aggressive and decisive. You actively pursue goals and targets and are energized by competitive situations. You always want to win and pay close attention to your competitors. You are a hard driver, very demanding of yourself and others. Speed, stealth, and discipline are key to your approach. You define success as energizing employees by expanding opportunities for problem solving and redeploying resources. You value power.

CHARACTERISTICS

You tend to...
- Pursue key goals
- Aggressively strive to win
- Focus on competitors
- Redeploy resources
- Focus on strategic projects
- Overcome barriers
- Solve challenging problems
- Influence through logic

EXAMPLES

- Angela Merkel (Chancellor of Germany)
- Indra Nooyi (CEO of PepsiCo)
- Jamie Dimon (CEO of JPMorgan Chase)
- Tim Cook (CEO of Apple)

STRENGTHS

- Strategic, opportunistic
- Focused, self-motivated, ambitious
- Assertive, decisive, rational
- Skillful, competent, hard-working, persistent
- Fast, action-oriented
- Effective, reward others for performance

WEAKNESSES

- Single-minded to achieve goals, can be ruthless
- Self-centered
- Short-sighted, overlook long-term implications
- Aggressive, domineering
- Workaholic, overworked, burn-out
- Uncollaborative, not inclusive

SKILLS TO DEVELOP

I. Take a Long-Term View
Hitting short-term goals is admirable, but you cannot forget your long-term plan: your vision in 5, 10, or even 20 years. Sustainable success means that you need to develop relationships and deep skills. Dedicate time to your pursuit, even if the rewards will be delayed.

2. Be Flexible to Accommodate Changes
In focusing fully on your goals, you may miss other, better ideas and targets. Instead of seeing with tunnel vision, elicit opinions from your peers and other professionals. Pay specific attention to those who have succeeded before you. Don't just look for opinions that confirm your own—challenge yourself. Open up your mind to possibilities.

3. Be a Better Team Player
Because you can be aggressive and competitive, people may find you difficult and prefer not to work with you. You can also prematurely dismiss people you judge as incompetent. Learn to show others that you care, and develop respect for others. You may be able to get things done more efficiently with the help of others.

HOW TO TALK TO AN ATHLETE

- Be logical and analytical
- Get to the point and summarize for others
- Show personal ownership
- Critically confront the downside of things
- Demonstrate a bias towards action

	IF YOU ARE AN ATHLETE	IF YOUR ORGANIZATION IS AN ATHLETE
THEN...	You will create value through your ability to get things done quickly and by meeting prescribed metrics.	Value is created when it shows superior performance against others.
AND YOU WORK WITH ARTISTS	Your relationship with them will succeed when there is a mutual emphasis on generating attention (or cheerleading) for a common visible project.	Your organization will successfully create value with others when the partnership generates capital for large, visible, and highly innovative projects.

FIGURE 4. **THE ATHLETE (continued on next page)**

FIGURE 4. **THE ATHLETE (continued from previous page)**

AND YOU WORK WITH ENGINEERS	Your relationship with them will succeed when there is a mutual interest in minimizing some sort of risk.	Your organization will successfully create value with others through key projects with clear goals, timelines, responsibilities, and outcomes.
AND YOU WORK WITH SAGES	The difficulties in your relationship with them will center on matters of individual deadlines and responsibilities. Make sure to allow adequate time for positive communication and the discussion of responsibilities, but take a leading role in setting reasonable targets and deliverables.	Your organization will have a difficult time because of a disagreement over matters of speed toward completion as well as specific project objectives. Set realistic objectives and deadlines that balance the need for speed with the need to learn what works and what doesn't work while maintaining strong communication.

Summary

The Athlete is always competitive, looking to produce the best work possible. Driven and relentless, they plow through barriers. They can grow by learning to be team players and slowing down. Athletes could benefit deeply from making sure that they have support from key stakeholders and considering all the relevant facts before running full tilt.

Exercise

Just as it's important that Artists and Engineers practice thinking more like the other, so too do Athletes and Sages need to exchange strategies. To make your ideas and plans more collaborative, try cultivating and accommodating the possibilities by asking the following *COLLABORATE* questions:

- **C**ooperate: What can we do to establish a shared culture?
- **O**pen: What can we do to be more inclusive?
- **L**isten: What can we do to better understand each other?
- **L**earn: What can we do to develop our skills or improve our abilities?
- **A**ttentive: What can we do to help others around us?
- **B**ridge: What can we do to resolve disagreements?
- **O**utreach: What can we do to support other communities?
- **R**espect: What can we do to treat others fairly?
- **A**ccommodate: What can we do to adapt to the circumstances?
- **T**rust: What can we do to demonstrate our commitment?
- **E**mpower: What can we do to give others the freedom and power to decide?

CHAPTER 9

The Sage

Mae loved to knit, but she didn't like beautiful things. Elegant and chic were two words not in her vocabulary. "If you want something that's in style, go to a store," she joked when relatives and friends gave her their requests for tasteful scarves and fashionable hats. Her specialty was tastelessness. Homespun kitsch—the kind of sweaters people wear ironically to ugly sweater parties—those were Mae's favorite pieces to make. She found beauty in the awful and was determined to share it with everyone she knew.

There was a sweet logic to Mae's preference for the ugly: in her eyes, the aesthetics of knitting were an afterthought. It was the connections she made with others that she valued most about her favorite pastime. In over 30 years of knitting every day, Mae forgot many of her most hideous creations, but she never forgot any of the people she made them for.

A social worker who constantly went out of her way to help others, Mae made her passion communal. In her living room, she hosted all sorts of friends, acquaintances, friends of friends—anyone with the slightest connection to knitting, from veteran knitters, to eager beginners, to reluctant recipients of future ugly sweaters. At her gatherings, she did what she did best: knitted and talked. While she stitched away, she listened to other people's problems, offered advice, and helped visitors find other people who might help them solve their problems.

Mae created much more than too many ugly sweaters to count. Her house became a kind of community center where people could chat, meet others, unwind, recharge, find solace, and, of course, knit.

Like a child outgrowing her baby quilt, Mae's weekly meetings got too large for her house. Eager to keep her at-home community center going, she looked around for other spaces. A nearby elementary school had recently become vacant. She'd heard rumors of an imminent demolition, so she went to the school board and asked if she could rent the space. Mae promised to keep the school in good condition and to pay a fee for the use of the space in return for the creation of an actual community center. The officials thought the idea was great and agreed to let Mae rent the space.

The knitting meet-up was only one of many regular activities at the new center. People of all ages, with interests of all kinds, showed up for a variety of programs, including open counseling groups and courses in painting, crafts, creative writing, and languages. Eventually, Mae let new teachers, mentors, and leaders run the center, and she enjoyed the facility as just another individual.

At the peak of the center's popularity and success, Mae died. In the wake of her absence—a huge devastation to everyone in the community—the center thrived. Instead of falling apart, the members, who all had different skills and specialties, stepped up and carried on Mae's legacy. The connoisseur of ugly had left behind a thing of surprising splendor.

A Compassionate
Facilitator

Part connector, part listener, part counselor, Mae is a Sage for the ages, a mentor even to other mentors. In her radiant—indeed, contagious—warmth, she's a shining example of this most compassionate of creative leaders. Her greatest qualities are the things that define Sages at the top of their games: persistence, empathy, and the desire, above all else, to be around, work with, and learn from both like-minded and totally different people.

Sages are facilitators that put everyone they meet at ease. They attract people and bring them together, creating a family atmosphere and collaborative spirit. Their charisma lies in their reserve, their willingness to let other people speak. Recall the way Mae gladly gave up her role heading up the community center once it got off the ground and she herself became an eager patron. Sages thrive on building a culture—defining the larger character and vision of the people they unite. They are the fundamental source of knowledge for the groups and teams they lead. They are the people who first develop the crucial competences and capabilities that endure for years or even lifetimes.

At the organizational level, the Sage companies are driven by their shared values—often by a desire to help others. They look for input from everyone within and without their ranks, from new and old employees, to consumers, to friends, and they welcome people of all kinds into their family. Think universities. Think Habitat for Humanity. Think Doctors Without Borders. This is a dynastic kind of innovation—a vision that gets passed down from generation to generation.

Example:
A Museum Changes
Its Culture

It is precisely this kind of lasting vision that one small Midwestern art museum needed to update as it adapted to a world changing much faster than it was. This is the story of a museum that needed to listen to its Sages. For this museum, innovation was about not merely questioning the rules of the institution but also reimagining the very definition of art itself.

This once-vibrant museum that had played a major role in the cultural and economic life of its community was quickly losing relevance, and its building had fallen into disarray. The directors needed to find a way to both raise money to repair the building and to regain the institution's artistic reputation.

At the center of this crisis was a large source of money that the museum couldn't use: a giant trust that had been established by donors in the early nineteenth century, with the stipulation that these funds be used solely for the acquisition of new art. So the current museum directors simply weren't allowed to tap into the trust to renovate the building or develop new education initiatives. This was a deeply hierarchical institution. Everyone had their own designated responsibilities, which rarely overlapped, and only a very small group of people had a real influence when it came to change.

The museum eventually put together cross-functional innovation teams that paired staff members with local volunteers and community leaders. The jumpstart sessions—mediated by Sages—were energetic and empowering, generating many great ideas.

But when it came to actually carrying out these ideas, the curator—an old bowtie-wearing, Ivy League–educated man—

shot everything down. "We can't do that," he said to nearly all the plans. The similarly conservative chairman of the board sided with the curator. With this standstill, there wasn't much they could do.

Then, something curious happened at the other side of the country. The news came out that a well-known, prestigious East Coast historical society was going under. Instead of selling a few of its valuable artifacts, the group chose to shut down its exhibition space and warehouse all its treasures because its directors believed that the central role of a historical society is to preserve art for studying and not to exhibit it to the hoi polloi.

Back in the Midwest, the curator took the position of the historical society directors. He thought that they did the right thing in closing their doors. He, too, thought that fine art was meant to be studied by trained scholars, not appreciated by an uninformed public.

This sparked a vibrant discussion among the museum directors about the fundamental role of art in the world. The deputy director—a younger man (a Sage) committed to making art accessible to as many people as possible—took a meeting with one of the most famous museums on the East Coast. He had the idea to organize a traveling exhibition of his own museum's collection of the Dutch Masters. It just so happened that this small, underdog museum in the Midwest had one of the world's top collections of seventeenth-century Dutch painters.

The curator didn't want to see these paintings on the road. He claimed there was too much risk in protecting these works in transit and that it would cost too much money to insure them. Here was the deputy director's way in: the giant nineteenth-century trust may not have provided funds for renovating the building, but it did make provisions for exhibitions. So the museum could use that money to insure the paintings.

The traveling exhibit was a major financial and cultural success. Soon, people from all over the globe came to this small Midwestern city to see these world-class masterpieces they couldn't see anywhere else. With this new income, the museum reestablished its relevance to the community, rebuilding its facilities and launching new education programs for underprivileged children. The Sage-like emphasis on reaching out to new audiences and celebrating the vitality of community is what saved this museum.

The deputy director—the Sage behind this breakthrough innovation—went on to take a position as the head of the major museum association, becoming a kind of cultural hero for small museums everywhere. The traveling exhibition is now a commonplace form of sharing work for a wider viewership and gaining aesthetic and fiscal capital for less-known institutions.

The Old Guard is not your enemy. Here, the curator was not a bad person—he was merely attached to a preexisting set of rules—a sacred cow—that needed to be updated. It wasn't about antagonizing him. It was about navigating him through the changing world we all shared, communicating with him and others, like a good Sage, and creating a new sense of community (and a new vision behind that community).

Patience:
The Sage's Greatest Gift and Downfall

The greatest asset of Sages is also their downfall: their patience. The kind of growth Sages seek is very slow. It can even take a generation to develop. In following the long timeline, Sages can miss out on the more immediate opportunities for advancement. It is for this reason that Sages must turn to Athletes as they plan their enduring projects. In this role, Athletes become more like coaches, keeping their team focused on the game that Sages like to forget they're even playing.

But in their avoidance of the game for the bigger picture, Sages are onto something. The sustainable culture that they work hard to develop—the set of customs and worldview that underlie the way an organization defines itself—is actually what ultimately drives the kind of success that Athletes crave. What Sages show us is that culture creates the economics of innovation.

Innovation Starts with
Mentorship

The key to building culture is the Sage's go-to mode of expression and connection: mentorship. Culture is about modeling and passing down core ideas and approaches. It involves apprenticing, nurturing, and teaching others. The teaching skills of a Sage are crucial to the success of any organization. For the innovation war room is less like a boardroom and more like a classroom: a place where leaders must perpetually learn new things about the ever-changing landscape of their industries. All innovation initiatives ask us to grapple with what we don't know now. That's why, when it comes to growth and creativity, learning is so important—and challenging.

Any Sage call tell you that teaching someone a skill is a lot easier than teaching someone how to apply that skill. Take a quick look at recent book sales, and this immediately becomes clear. This past summer, booksellers reported abysmally low numbers.

We spend thirteen years and billions of dollars teaching children how to read, but studies show us that, once they leave school, a quarter of people don't read a single book in a year. Knowing how to read is not the same thing as wanting to read—or knowing how to apply the information and insights gained from reading.

The other major challenge to learning that Sages know well is one that transcends time and age: whether you're eight or eighty, a PhD or a GED, if you want to acquire a new skill, you have to go through the failure cycle. We are all novices when it comes to entering the unknown—and we have to be ready and willing to endure early mistakes and missteps.

With new technologies arising faster than we can keep up with and constant changes in the culture of the workforce and customer preferences, it's not enough to be learners. We need to *re*learn how we take in and respond to new skills and ideas. We all have to be Sages to ourselves and to those around us.

Learn How
You Learn

It's time to learn how you learn. Cultivate a self-awareness about your learning process. In the 1960s, Berkeley professors Richard Bandler and John Grinder developed a cognitive inquiry strategy called Neuro-Linguistic Programming that many still use today. The approach claims that there are three types of learning: auditory, visual, and kinesthetic. Howard Gardner, a famous developmental psychologist at Harvard, takes this one step further, insisting that we actually have multiple intelligences: visual-spatial, bodily-kinesthetic, musical, interpersonal, intrapersonal, linguistic, and logical-mathematical. Pay attention to when things make the most sense for you. What is the first thing you do whenever you're trying to understand a new concept? Do you learn by reading instructions? By watching someone else do it? Or by listening to someone explain it? Knowing your own learning strengths is not just about yourself—it will also help you communicate with others. All effective leaders teach in multiple modalities and realize that one way of explaining something won't be understood by an entire group.

We need to be sensitive to where people are in their development of a skill. We can't just jump from the first step to the final step. Bring learners along slowly through each stage. Have acknowledged masters apprentice novices. Masters aren't always senior leaders. They might be young people who are fluent in new technology or people who have little formal education but have extensive life experience.

Embrace the patience of a Sage and give learning time. All learning is developmental. Speak a foreign language or pick up a musical instrument, and you'll see that there are no shortcuts. We all need immersion and soak time. Increase your tolerance for failure. Consider the two basic kinds of parents—the ones who say, "Don't do that," and the ones who say, "Hurt, didn't it?" The children of the hovering parents likely won't learn as much as the ones who have the freedom to do things. The only time we don't say, "Hurt, didn't it?" is when the child is in peril. Ask yourself what kind of leader you are: do you let the people around you fail—or are you stopping them from experimenting in the first place? Make learning a team sport.

Pair different kinds of learners together and bring together varying levels—and areas—of expertise. Establish an everyday culture of learning by modeling the learning behaviors you want to see in your team. Show curiosity. Ask questions. Share what you know. Remember that the innovation classroom has no start date and no end date. When it comes to creativity and growth, the Sage knows best: class is always in session.

The Beauty of
Collaborative Innovation

A culture of everyday learning is the new normal. In many ways, the Sage's perspective dominates our current creative landscape where collaboration and the perpetual drive to learn more reign supreme. Collaboration has recently emerged as the defining characteristic of creativity and growth in nearly all sectors and industries. Today, the biggest breakthroughs happen when networks of self-motivated people with a collective vision join together and share ideas, information, and work.

Collaborative innovation comes in many forms and kinds. From brainstorming sessions like innovation jams to crowdfunding initiatives like Kickstarter or crowdsourcing initiatives like InnoCentive, these forms of growth all mobilize an assorted group of people with a range of skills. The benefits to joint innovation efforts are plenty: the global scale of the initiative, the rapidity of experimentation, the reservoirs of outside talent, and the guaranteed wider array of solutions.

But with each of these upsides also comes a downside: the chaos of implementation, the disruptive power of clients, the difficulty of serving solutions, and the uncertainty of constantly changing course. These are issues that Sages and all teams, at some level, struggle with. The challenge is to achieve equality without uniformity, variety without discord, and cooperation without consensus.

Exercise:
Build a Board of Advisors

In their constant desire for new and diverse voices, Sages are experts at gathering the perfect combination of people with different areas of expertise to provide counsel about important matters. This kind of board of advisors is something that both individual people and large-scale organizations could benefit from. Typically, boards of advisors provide sound advice, help secure resources, and connect you to other high-potential candidates. So it is wise to think like a Sage and continuously develop a manageable board of advisors, typically around seven people. Consider the following points when putting together your board of advisors:

1. To get a comprehensive set of perspectives, be sure to diversify your board of advisors with people from all four dominant worldviews:

   - Artists, who explore a wide range of imaginative possibilities and experiment with several of them simultaneously

   - Engineers, who review the data and develop detailed plans with sequential steps to resolve their challenges

   - Athletes, who eliminate all distractions and unnecessary projects and focus on a few key goals

   - Sages, who widen their social circle and discuss their challenges with others to learn if they have solutions that they can use

   Deep and diverse domain expertise is essential for a successful board of advisors because it increases our ability to produce constructive conflict and generate innovative solutions. Look for areas of expertise that are relevant to your aspirations. For example, if you intend to create a successful Internet blog, you might want to include someone on your board of advisors who already has a large following.

2. Establish some simple guidelines that encourage positive interactions and esprit de corps.

3. To help secure resources, you need to seek out those influential and powerful individuals whom you know as well as those whom you can come to know through your relationships and networks. Look for people who have shared aspirations and values:

   - Who wants the same type of things that you want?
   - Who has the means to move you closer to your aspirations?
   - What did these individuals seek?
   - How can working with you help them get what they seek?
   - What is the best way to reach out to them and enlist their support?

   Remember, this group of advisors may be engaged at different levels and change over time. Everyone doesn't contribute in the same way.

4. To enlist and enroll other high-potential candidates into the organization, first consider what others seek and stand to gain by joining in your community. The good news is that everyone wants something. The bad news is that they all want something different: satisfaction, knowledge, connections, prestige, or simply affiliation. Effective networks are complementary. There is something in it for everyone. When you approach potential members to join your board of advisors, consider the offer from their point of view and

think of what they want and what you can offer them. Be flexible and work to find a common ground where everyone stands to win from the collaboration.

Once you have formed your initial board of advisors, regularly reach out to them with questions and requests for support and seek out their advice. In return, be supportive to them whenever possible. Encourage the expression of diverse views but work to keep the tension positive. Most of all, work to develop a trusting professional relationship and establish personal rapport. Over time, members of your board of advisors may change as your needs and theirs change.

Keep challenging yourself and those around you to go outside of the limits and boundaries that other people take for granted as fixed or insurmountable. Change up the ways you communicate with others. Pull a Mae and break free of your living room to scope out new locations. Any building has the potential to become the next community center.

The Sage

DESCRIPTION

As a Sage, you are empathetic. You care for other people, whether they are your family or colleagues. You are skilled at building a community of people and sharing knowledge between them. You seek interaction among community members and allies; therefore you use processes such as conflict management and consensus decision making as a means. Your success is defined by the creation of strong relationships through dialog, trust, and understanding. Outcomes of these collaborative practices are shared values and commitment. You use your team orientation and cooperative nature to accomplish your goals.

CHARACTERISTICS

You tend to...
- Develop people
- Manage relationships
- Build community
- Pursue commitment
- Manage conflict
- Seek consensus
- Influence through empowerment
- Facilitate learning

EXAMPLES

- Jimmy Wales (CEO of Wikipedia)
- Jack Ma (CEO of Alibaba)
- Geoffrey Canada (President of the Harlem Children's Zone)
- Mary Barra (CEO of General Motors)

STRENGTHS

- Sensitive, caring, helpful
- Empowering, inclusive
- Open-minded to differing opinions
- Resolve conflicts, gain consensus
- Build commitment and trust
- Like to learn and teach others

WEAKNESSES

- Slow to act
- Unassertive
- Too much reliance on teamwork
- Let emotion overrule logic
- Unclear in direction
- Lack focus to hit targets and goals

1. Get Things Done—Pick Up the Pace
You can spend a long time in eliciting participation, resolving conflicts, and creating a cohesive community. However, you also need to be mindful of your goals and the time constraints. Develop more disciplines, set milestones, and follow them to get things done faster.

2. Use More Logic and Facts
Be more decisive and prepare yourself to make tough and unpopular choices. Use hard facts and data as one variable in your decision-making process. Don't choose a solution just because it fits your values. Choose it because it is the most effective course of action.

3. Be More Assertive, Clear, and Direct
You may be uncomfortable in criticizing others or in voicing your opinion when it differs from everyone else's. However, the different opinion may be what everybody needs. Express yourself clearly, and do not worry too much about offending other people or sounding demanding. Give critical but loving and supportive feedback to other people in your life.

HOW TO TALK TO A SAGE

- Share personal experiences, express emotions, be open
- Be friendly, put people at ease
- Think out loud
- Understand the importance of intuition
- Use non-verbal gestures

	IF YOU ARE A SAGE	**IF YOUR ORGANIZATION IS A SAGE**
THEN...	You will create value through your commitment to teaching and mentoring others.	Value is created when human capital and organizational learning create sustainable competitive advantage.
AND YOU WORK WITH ENGINEERS	Your relationship with them will succeed when you place a collective emphasis on learning to do things the right way.	Your organization will successfully create value with others through building long-term relationships that build industry knowledge.

FIGURE 5. **THE SAGE (continued on next page)**

FIGURE 5. **THE SAGE (continued from previous page)**

AND YOU WORK WITH ARTISTS	Your relationship with them will succeed when you collectively try new things, generate new ideas, and mutually learn what works and what doesn't work in a supportive manner.	Your organization will successfully create value with others through innovative, long-term partnerships to generate new knowledge.
AND YOU WORK WITH ATHLETES	The difficulties in your relationship with them will center on matters of individual deadlines and responsibilities. Make sure to let the others set deadlines, but take a leading role in clarifying details and encouraging positive communication about mutual responsibilities.	Your organization will have a difficult time because of a disconnect over matters of speed toward completion as well as specific objectives. Set realistic objectives and deadlines that balance the need for speed with the need to learn what works and what doesn't work while maintaining strong communication.

Summary

Warm, compassionate, and natural extroverts, Sages love to work in teams and collaborate with other people. They build connections, relationships, and communities. They can grow by learning to assert themselves, avoiding groupthink, and allowing logic to guide their decisions instead of just emotions.

Exercise

Stretch out the possibilities of Sage-motivated innovation by subjecting your community-building impulses to the more cutthroat attitude of an Athlete. To make your ideas and plans more competitive, try accelerating and focusing the possibilities by asking the following *COMPETE* questions:

- **C**hallenge: What can we do to win?
- **O**vercome: What can we do to break through our obstacles to success?
- **M**aneuver: What can we do to outsmart our competitors?
- **P**ush: What can we do to move faster?
- **E**nergize: What can we do to excite our team?
- **T**arget: What can we do to focus on the results?
- **E**ngage: What can we do to meet our rivals head-on?

CHAPTER 10

When Athletes and Sages Meet: An Exercise in Constructive Conflict

Athletes are extremely competitive and quickly pursue their goals. Sages are directed by their values and their interest in developing a harmonious community. While Athletes are better at capturing opportunities as they emerge, Sages are more effective at building the culture and competencies necessary to sustain these gains. So the key to simultaneously maximizing the benefits from both dominant worldviews is to identify the most winning members of your team and then to make their practices a part of the team's underlying culture, codifying their gifts by using them as criteria for hiring and staffing.

Competitive organizations such as sports franchises or celebrated restaurants use scouting reports to assess high-potential talent. A great quarterback or a world-renowned chef can be the difference between success and failure. While individual performance is essential, how a player fits within the mission and strategy of an organization is equally as important. This is where the Athlete and the Sage share a common aim but with a vastly different approach.

Follow this exercise to create a dynasty of winning teams:

1. Identify clear goals for success. These can be quantifiable, such as a 10 percent increase in profits next year, or qualitative, such as adherence to an oath of service.

2. Investigate which performers currently have the best track record in achieving this goal. This person can be within your organization or another organization. Gather information like an anthropologist working in the field. Analyze the information as if you were an intelligence officer or an industry analyst.

3. Based on your investigation, set two sets of realistic benchmarks for performance. The first set of benchmarks should be measurable targets or key indicators, for example:

   - Reduce our operating budget by 5 percent by the start of next month
   - Lower employee attrition rates by 30 percent by the end of next year
   - Accelerate our time to market for new product development by seven days

The second set of benchmarks should be specific performance or demonstrated ability that you want, for example, the ability to:

- Build and lead teams
- Create a broad coalition of support
- Implement easy and early wins

4. Connect the two sets of benchmarks: the measurable goal with the performance attributes that create them to develop a scorecard by which to measure and assess potential high performers. See the example below:

- Goal: To achieve lower employee attrition rates by 30 percent by the end of next year
- Performance Attributes: Rate the candidates on their ability to perform the tasks listed below (Table 6)

	Create a Broad Coalition of Support			Develop a Strategy to Overcome Barriers to Teamwork			Establish a Positive Culture of Continuous Learning		
CANDIDATES	H	M	L	H	M	L	H	M	L
1									
2									
3									

TABLE 6. **RATING THE CANDIDATES**

5. Connect the dots by applying this scorecard in many processes, such as an interview process, a new employee orientation program, team-building exercises, or other organizational development systems.

6. Fully integrate the desired attributes into your training and mentoring program to develop these skills in your current employees. For example, you might want to pair an Athlete and a Sage in a workshop on effective teambuilding. Depending upon their abilities, you may also want to include these high performers as trainers, facilitators, and coaches.

By searching for high performers and reapplying their best practices to the appropriate members of the organization, you can reach quick and sustainable innovation through the constructive conflict between the Athlete and Sage.

CHAPTER 11

The Innovation Code Within

Patrick wanted to be a professor. His dreams went beyond ivy-covered campuses and comfortable offices with overflowing bookshelves. Although his interests in the somber poetry of English medieval martyrs were even more obscure than those of his grad student cohort's, his aspirations were bigger. He didn't want to become just another charming tweed-wearing colleague at a faculty party talking incessantly about some arcane factoid only two other people in the world knew or cared about. He imagined becoming the kind of broad-minded raconteur whose musings are accessible to anyone and everyone—the sort of public intellectual with ideas that transcend the limits of discipline.

When Patrick got into a PhD program at a top university known for cross-boundary collaboration, he had the hope and eagerness of a lovesick schoolboy. He left all his friends and family in Los Angeles for the cozy Midwestern college town.

But he quickly found that, when it came to his personal and intellectual odyssey, other people were in control. The only thing Patrick chose his entire first year in grad school was the apartment he lived in. Everything else was decided by his advisors and the director of graduate studies: the courses he took, the books he wrote about, the research he did over the summer.

Incensed, Patrick felt misled. He'd come to the university to develop his own ideas but instead found himself institutionalized against his will. With the norms, expectations, and culture of the academic community forcibly imposed on him, he felt suffocated. Resistant and recalcitrant, Patrick argued with authorities, complained to friends, and took long walks to cool off. The Man was holding him down.

Through a mutual acquaintance, Patrick met a professor in the sociology department who seemed to be the antithesis of his own advisors. Professor Barry was always on a jet somewhere for a conference or at meetings with people who wanted to hear his ideas and apply them to sectors totally outside of academia. Barry wrote weird, wild articles for mainstream magazines and had just signed a book contract with a high-profile press. Patrick became Barry's research assistant. Barry hated the title, but research assistantships were the only way for faculty to get university money to pay grad students for mentorship pairings. Patrick helped Barry on emerging projects and traveled around the country with him to conferences and meetings with industry leaders.

Three months into their partnership, Patrick confided to Barry that he hoped to have a kaleidoscopic career just like his one day. "Then you'd better start doing what your advisors are telling you to do," he said. The senior scholar's reply shocked Patrick.

What Patrick didn't see was the horizon in front of him. He didn't realize that he needed to endure these three years of required course work and sit for his preliminary examinations—a medieval process of glorified hazing that was in many ways more barbaric than the stuff Patrick read in his eleventh-century poems—in order to be successful when he'd finally get the independence he always wanted. In these difficult three years, Patrick had to develop the academic skills and the disciplines he needed to grow into the broad-minded intellectual with interesting ideas. He had to see the world through different lenses in order to gain more understanding of and further develop himself.

Once he got through these unpleasant milestones, Patrick had three years of complete freedom to write the dissertation of his dreams—a scholarly book of original ideas. His advisors stopped telling him what to do and started encouraging him to follow his own interests. Beyond the point where he had to answer to authority, he assumed authority over his own project. He reached out to people in other departments, other schools, and nonacademic publishing houses and magazines and talked with intellectuals and well-worn practitioners about his ideas. Then something strange started to happen. The more Patrick followed the flow of ideas, the more his point of view began to blend with others, and soon new and greater concepts emerged. A deeper understanding appeared in his research and writing, and his dissertation was very well received.

Still, there were tacit rules and protocols he needed to follow. In order to get accepted into the top journal of his field, he had to tone down his usually animated style. But once his first few scholarly articles got recognition in the discipline, he got more traction with more popular publications. As he settled into a teaching job at a small liberal arts school—far from the kind of research institution he imagined ending up at—he gradually built a reputation in academic and nonacademic circles alike. His second book became a surprise crossover best seller, and he eventually transitioned into teaching part-time to devote full energy to his career as a public intellectual.

Patrick was an Artist with the drive of an Athlete surrounded by Sages and Engineers. But to achieve the kind of life he wanted, he needed to turn on—and off—all of the various switches of the Innovation Code at different times. At the onset of his graduate years, he had to suck it up and hunker down like an Engineer. As he prepared for his preliminary examinations, he embraced his Athletic side, his eyes on the prize. While he wrote his dissertation and reached out to scholars working on similar projects, he took on the role of a Sage. And, all the while, he stayed true to his fundamental identity and vision as an Artist.

We All Have Every
Dominant Worldview

At some level, despite our dominant worldviews, we have the qualities of all four Innovation Code archetypes within us. The dynamics of the Innovation Code are not just at work in teams and organizations but also in individuals. You might be a Sage, an Athlete, an Artist, or an Engineer, but you also have some tendencies of all the other kinds of thinking, feeling, and problem-solving. We can let all of these conflicting impulses create havoc and anxiety—or we can use them to harness productivity. Getting the kind of holistic life we all seek is a matter of turning on and off select qualities when we need them the most, even if they sometimes go against our usual way of doing things.

Think of your identity like a team of different thinkers, with separate interests that need to be prioritized (and de-emphasized) at the appropriate moments. Managing your inner team is a constant rebalancing of all these various identities. So rather than embodying the extremity of your dominant worldview, become a Sage, Athlete, Engineer, or Artist when the occasion calls for it.

You might be flirting with an old entrepreneurial idea, a lifelong dream that you're considering to give up your present career for. Or maybe you're a recently retired doctor boomeranging back into a medical practice because fishing and golf just aren't enough for you. Or maybe it's your twenty-five-year old daughter who is trying to reinvent herself after her hitch with the Peace Corps by going back to school for her MBA. We all seem to be chasing something we haven't got or moving the bar once we get "there."

Reshuffling Your
Inner Team

Try reshuffling your inner team. Remember Aabha the Engineer? It turns out she taps into her inner Artist every day by keeping a notebook for creative ideas and maintaining a lifelong interest in spirituality. She visits holy places of all religions wherever she travels.

Remember Mae the Sage? She nourished her inner Athlete and her hunger for competition by showing up for a daily appointment with herself to work out. Her aggressive side came out on a regular basis as she actively managed her investments.

Remember Gary the Athlete? He feeds his Sage side and his instinct to collaborate by cultivating his curiosity and exposing himself to both like-minded and diverse thinkers. He seeks out new experts and enrolls in continuing education courses. He also recognizes that staying connected to family, friends, and community keeps his collaborative capabilities sharp and in focus. Last year he went on a camping trip with his family—perhaps the greatest test of one's sagacity (and patience).

Remember Tom the Artist? He can be quite the Engineer. His need to maintain some control over his life has led him to institute small rituals: he keeps a cash jar for family emergencies and, as a way to satisfy his desire for productivity, he also occasionally volunteers for projects that will enhance him professionally, even if they don't pay.

Take the
Long View

Like any high-performance team, take the long view of your projects. This means that what you do, and the changes you might make, must reflect what you believe you really want at any given time. So you may pursue very different types of outcomes in various areas of your life. For example, you might be an Artist by traveling to Bhutan, while also being an Engineer by moving some of your investments out of the volatile market and into a savings account. Over time, you will recognize a rhythm to these patterns in your life: compartmentalizing demands and desires into the four archetypes of the Innovation Code may actually free you up to pursue the wildest of options.

Patrick's story goes on, with an even more diversified life. Twelve years after he got his first job, he is married with two children. Some weeks it's about the kids: karate, violin, catechism, and the like. Some weeks it's about the career: travel to conferences, lectures, academic papers, and so on. Every Sunday he and his wife sit down and talk about their lives. They shift things around, create hybrid solutions, and connect a lot of dots. With a little luck, most of the time, their life is reasonably balanced, and for that they are grateful.

Imagine if your dreams came true the day you graduated from high school: the bright lights of Broadway, a fast car, a happily-ever-after engagement to the beautiful homecoming king or queen. Would you still be happy today? While some might be, many of us have outgrown our early dreams and have new ones to pull us forward. So, as you're planning your way to the future, why not leave a little room for the things you don't know now? Diversify your life to hedge against unforeseen challenges and give yourself the freedom to pursue emerging opportunities. That way you can have it all when you really want to have it.

Summary

Beneath your dominant worldview lies all the other Innovation Code archetypes: we all have an inner Artist, Engineer, Athlete, and Sage, pushing and pulling against each other as different threads of our characters. Just as you would at the organizational level, use that inner tension to create something powerful. It is in our inconsistencies and opposing impulses where we will find ways to do newer and better things.

Exercise

Return to the stories of failure and success you told about yourself—and examined—at the end of Chapters One, Three, and Four. Now, with that same reflective, self-challenging attitude, tell a story of your *future,* a story of something you want to achieve. Incorporate the simple rules of thumb you gleaned from your earlier stories of failure and success to plan the way you'll approach your target. Ask yourself these questions:

- What will I stop doing this time?
- What will I start doing this time?
- What will I keep doing this time?
- What will I change about the way I see myself, others, and my target?

Our stories are iterative. Like us, they are works in progress. Continue to tell your story, but keep modifying both the story itself and the way you tell it until it feels authentic. This will give you real insight into your biggest weaknesses, your biggest strengths, and how to use both as you navigate your way through your forward-looking story of soon-to-be-success.

The Innovation Code
Supplemental
Material

To help deepen your understanding about the Innovation Code and how to create constructive conflicts, we have prepared additional material for you and your team, such as:

1. The Innovation Code Simple Quiz

This is a quick online version of the quiz you find at the end of Chapter Two. It tabulates your responses automatically so you do not need any pens or pencils.

2. The Innovation Code Self-Assessment

This premium assessment takes about 15 minutes to complete and measures your dominant worldview and that of your organization or team. You will receive a comprehensive report that shows you not just how you innovate but also how you can contribute the most to your team and most importantly, how you can create constructive conflicts effectively. Bulk-order discounts are available so that you and your entire team organization can take this assessment.

3. The Innovation Code Card Game

This deck of cards is a fun way to spend time with your team, family, or friends to figure out your and their dominant worldviews. It's a great way to get to know each other better and as a team bonding exercise. The deck comes with 52 cards and a set of instructions.

4. How to Create a High-Performing Team Kit

Teams are works in progress. You need to find the right combination of people by first figuring out what you are good at (and bad at) and then finding people who can complement your skills. Your team should provide enough diversity to allow for a healthy exchange of ideas and creative conflicts, but it should be cohesive enough with a sense of purpose. This kit helps you put together the right team for your innovation project and comes with interview questions and surveys to pick the right members for what you need. It also comes with a few guides to resolve negative conflicts and harness the constructive conflicts.

Please visit www.bkconnection.com/innovationcode for these and other material we have developed.

Index

Note: an *f* indicates a figure; a *t*, a table.

Acknowledgments

Thank you to Logan Scherer for your brilliance, diligence, and craft in making this book happen.

Thank you to our publisher extraordinaire Steve Piersanti and the entire Berrett-Koehler family for bringing this book to life.

Thank you to Robert Quinn and Kim Cameron for building the theoretical foundation upon which this work rests.

Authors' Notes

All stories and examples in this book, either about a specific person or organization, are based on our decades of work consulting with Fortune 500 companies. Details such as name, gender, occupation, location, and certain facts have been altered for purposes of privacy, confidentiality, and ethics. Some stories are composites or have been changed to better illustrate the business issues.

About the Authors

Jeff DeGraff has an unorthodox approach to life. A professor at the Ross School of Business, at the University of Michigan, his life is full of the twists and turns of an innovator. A true Artist,★ he has tried things, faced failures and successes, and charted his own course, continually looking at what's beyond the horizon. Inspired by Walt Disney, he follows the mantra "Keep moving forward."

Having gained his doctorate degree in just two years when he was only 25, Jeff turned down an academic position at a prestigious Ivy League university only to become the youngest executive at the fastest-growing pizza company in the 1980s. He then combined the world of academia with the world of business to emerge as an engaging and highly sought-after professor, speaker, and consultant. His client list reads as a "Who's Who" within the world of innovators, including, among many others, General Electric, Coca-Cola, American College of Surgeons, and Google. Jeff's creative and direct take on making innovation really happen has made him a world-renowned thought leader and prompted his clients and colleagues to dub him as the "Dean of Innovation."

Jeff's mission is "the democratization of innovation." He brings innovation to everyone, every day, and everywhere through his books (such as *Making Stone Soup*), his public television program (*Innovation You*), columns (*Inc.*) and radio program (*The Next Idea*). To learn more, please visit www.jeffdegraff.com.

Staney DeGraff is one of the main sources of constructive conflicts in Jeff's life. Being an innate Athlete,★ she developed the Sage★ part of herself while being raised in a Chinese family in Indonesia. As a result, she loves managing projects and building communities. While Jeff gets things started, Staney translates things into reality and moves them to the next step.

Staney makes things work. She directs the Innovatrium (www.innovatrium.org), an innovation institute, and manages the consulting practice. She works with the College of Engineering at the University of Michigan to bring the Certified Professional Innovator program (CPInnovator.com) to all would-be innovators everywhere. With both an MBA and a Masters in Computer Science and Engineering, she designed and developed the award-winning Collaborative Innovation Network for the University of Michigan staff.

About the Authors

Staney's research and consulting focus is on developing organizational culture and practices that make innovation work and endure. She is a committed educator who is constantly creating new ways for people with diverse backgrounds and points of view to collaborate successfully.

Jeff and Staney have been married and working together for decades. Staney understands that Jeff has to spout new ideas every other day, and Jeff is resigned that some of his ideas only make sense to him. They live in Ann Arbor with an assortment of children and pets that are treated like children. They enjoy travel, theater, and Michigan football.

---

*The Artist, Engineer, Sage, and Athlete are the four dominant worldviews that can generate constructive conflicts described in this book.

Berrett–Koehler
BK Publishers

Berrett-Koehler is an independent publisher dedicated to an ambitious mission: *Connecting people and ideas to create a world that works for all.*

We believe that the solutions to the world's problems will come from all of us, working at all levels: in our organizations, in our society, and in our own lives. Our BK Business books help people make their organizations more humane, democratic, diverse, and effective (we don't think there's any contradiction there). Our BK Currents books offer pathways to creating a more just, equitable, and sustainable society. Our BK Life books help people create positive change in their lives and align their personal practices with their aspirations for a better world.

All of our books are designed to bring people seeking positive change together around the ideas that empower them to see and shape the world in a new way.

And we strive to practice what we preach. At the core of our approach is Stewardship, a deep sense of responsibility to administer the company for the benefit of all of our stakeholder groups including authors, customers, employees, investors, service providers, and the communities and environment around us. Everything we do is built around this and our other key values of quality, partnership, inclusion, and sustainability.

This is why we are both a B-Corporation and a California Benefit Corporation—a certification and a for-profit legal status that require us to adhere to the highest standards for corporate, social, and environmental performance.

We are grateful to our readers, authors, and other friends of the company who consider themselves to be part of the BK Community. We hope that you, too, will join us in our mission.

A BK Business Book

We hope you enjoy this BK Business book. BK Business books pioneer new leadership and management practices and socially responsible approaches to business. They are designed to provide you with groundbreaking and practical tools to transform your work and organizations while upholding the triple bottom line of people, planet, and profits. High-five!

To find out more, visit **www.bkconnection.com**.

Berrett–Koehler
Publishers

Connecting people and ideas
to create a world that works for all

Dear Reader,

Thank you for picking up this book and joining our worldwide community of Berrett-Koehler readers. We share ideas that bring positive change into people's lives, organizations, and society.

To welcome you, we'd like to offer you a free e-book. You can pick from among twelve of our bestselling books by entering the promotional code **BKP92E** here: http://www.bkconnection.com/welcome.

When you claim your free e-book, we'll also send you a copy of our e-newsletter, the *BK Communiqué*. Although you're free to unsubscribe, there are many benefits to sticking around. In every issue of our newsletter you'll find

- A free e-book
- Tips from famous authors
- Discounts on spotlight titles
- Hilarious insider publishing news
- A chance to win a prize for answering a riddle

Best of all, our readers tell us, "Your newsletter is the only one I actually read." So claim your gift today, and please stay in touch!

Sincerely,

Charlotte Ashlock
Steward of the BK Website

Questions? Comments? Contact me at bkcommunity@bkpub.com.